THE WORD OF
RECONCILIATION

*'God hath committed unto us
the Word of Reconciliation'*

THE WORD OF
RECONCILIATION

H. H. FARMER, D.D.

JAMES NISBET & CO. LTD
DIGSWELL PLACE
1966

Published by
James Nisbet & Co. Ltd
Digswell Place, Welwyn, Herts

First Published . . . 1966
Printed by Butler and Tanner Ltd
Frome and London

PREFACE

This book comprises lectures delivered on the Ayer Foundation of the Colgate Rochester Divinity School, Rochester, N.Y. in 1961. A good deal of the same material was incorporated in lectures delivered in the same year on the Earl Foundation of the Pacific School of Religion, Berkeley, California, and later in Knox College, Dunedin, and Ormond College, Melbourne. It gives me pleasure to acknowledge again the warm welcome which I received from the Presidents and Faculties of these schools on the occasion of the delivery of the lectures and throughout my stay among them. I cherish the happiest memories of this.

The lectures are here reproduced substantially as delivered except for emendations and additions which have been made in the light of subsequent discussion and reflection and in the light of comments made by the Reverend Professor C. F. D. Moule, Lady Margaret's Professor of Divinity in the University of Cambridge, who did me the honour of reading the lectures in manuscript and to whom I am, now as always, deeply indebted.

H. H. FARMER

Hove, Sussex
February 1966.

INTRODUCTION

This volume constitutes the Ayer Lectures for 1961. The Ayer Lectureship was founded in May 1928, in the Rochester Theological Seminary, by the gift of twenty-five thousand dollars from Mr and Mrs Wilfred W. Fry, of Camden, New Jersey, to perpetuate the memory of Mrs Fry's father, the late Mr Francis Wayland Ayer. At the time of his death Mr Ayer was president of the corporation which maintained the Rochester Theological Seminary.

Shortly after the establishment of the Lectureship the Rochester Theological Seminary and the Colgate Theological Seminary were united under the name of the Colgate Rochester Divinity School. It is under the auspices of this Institution that the Ayer Lectures are given.

Under the terms of the Foundation the lectures are to fall within the broad field of the history or interpretation of the Christian religion and message. It is the desire of those connected with the establishment and administration of the Lectureship that the lectures shall be religiously constructive and shall help in the building of Christian faith.

Four lectures are given each year at the Colgate Rochester Divinity School at Rochester, New York, and these lectures are published in book form. They are known as the Ayer Lectures.

The lecturer for the year 1961 was Professor Herbert H. Farmer.

CONTENTS

CHAPTER I

THE VOCATION OF CHRIST

(1)

THE purpose of these lectures is to consider, along certain broad lines, the saving work of Christ. If we were minded to use a technical theological term, we might say that the subject is to be 'soteriology', but though that would impart to the statement a mildly academic flavour it might also be a little misleading. For it is not our intention to engage in any thorough discussion of even a few of the deep theological problems which have arisen in the course of Christian reflection, through the centuries, on the saving work of our Lord, and which are usually subsumed under the term 'soteriology'. The importance of such problems is not to be minimized, but they are not here our prime concern. What I want to do is to go farther back, to get more to the experiential data out of which the theological problems arise and with which all discussion of them must keep in touch if it is not to go astray. Behind and beneath explanatory theories of Christ's work as Saviour there is the saving work itself, what he actually has done, and does, in the lives of men and women who, in the New Testament phrase, are 'being saved',[1] irrespective of whether they have formulated, or even are capable of formulating, some sort of satisfactory theory about it. Behind, so to say, the 'why' and the 'how' of Christ's

[1] I *Corinthians* I, 18; 2 *Corinthians* 2, 15.

work in men's lives is the 'what'. It is in the latter that we are here primarily interested.

Of course, this distinction between experience and theology must not be made in too absolute a way; the two always interpenetrate and affect one another. All religious experience has a good deal of implicit and un-formulated theology in it; on the other hand, a man's ex-plicit, formulated theology, if he has one, always tends to work back into his experience and may even in a mea-sure determine what sort of experience he is capable of having. Nevertheless, the distinction is always there and must be borne in mind; experience and the interpretation of experience are inseparable, but they are not the same, and a failure to realize that they are not the same has lain behind some unfortunate aspects and episodes of the Church's life and history in times past.

Our question then is, what does it mean to be a saved man, saved through Christ, to be the 'new man' in Christ —to *be* it livingly in oneself and in practice, and not merely to have second-order knowledge about it or an allegedly sound theology of it? What is it that distinctively charac-terizes, or should distinctively characterize, such a man, marks him off, for all his continuing faults and failings and sins, from those who are *not* so saved, not new men in Christ, and imparts to him in some observable measure a specifically Christ-style of life? And, further, how is this newness of life and character related to, derivative from, Christ, so that it is strictly true to say that it is given to a man through Christ alone, strictly true to describe it as the specifically Christ-style of life, there being in fact no other way succinctly to indicate both its quality and its source?

Central in the general title of these lectures is the

term 'reconciliation'—'The Word of Reconciliation'—and conformably with this the questions I have just formulated can be restated thus: what does it mean to *be* a reconciled man, reconciled through Christ? what distinctively characterizes the 'by-Christ-reconciled' man? and so on. My purpose in making the term 'reconciliation' thus central and dominant and the justification of it will, I hope, appear as we proceed. At the moment I would like to say three preliminary things.

First, the theme as I have just formulated it obviously brings us close to the heart of the New Testament. The New Testament speaks frequently in one way or another of newness of life bestowed on men by God through Christ.[2] And certainly it is all about 'reconciliation', even if that precise term is not often used. In one central passage the two ideas of 'newness of life' and 'reconciliation' are brought into close relation with one another. 'If any one is in Christ, he is a new creation; the old has passed away, behold, the new has come. All this is from God, who through Christ reconciled us to himself and gave us the ministry of reconciliation, that is, God was in Christ reconciling the world to himself.'[3]

Second, I am using the term 'reconciliation', and shall use it, in a rather more comprehensive sense than that in which it is sometimes used. I am using it to cover *all* the main aspects of Christ's saving work in men's lives, and therefore, derivatively from that, *all* the basic distinctive qualities of the new man in Christ. The term 'reconciliation' is not infrequently used to indicate only, or at least mainly, Christ's saving work in relation to the forgiveness

[2] *2 Corinthians* 5, 17 ff.; *Galatians* 6, 15; *Romans* 6, 4; 7, 6; *Ephesians* 4, 23–24.
[3] *2 Corinthians* 5, 17 ff. (R.S.V.). See also *Ephesians* 2, 14–20.

of sins, the bringing of a man in his sinfulness, and in spite of his sinfulness, into a new relation of fellowship with God with whom he otherwise stands because of his sinfulness in a relation of profound estrangement. In other words, it is often equated with 'atonement' in the sense in which that term is as a rule used in systematic theologies and histories of doctrine. But, as I have said, we here use the word 'reconciliation' in a wider sense, to cover all the main aspects of what Christ does savingly for the human spirit. According to this usage, 'atonement' in the narrower sense just indicated is but *one* aspect of Christ's total, all-inclusive work of reconciliation, the most important and fundamental aspect no doubt, but still but one aspect.

Third, thus to use the word 'reconciliation' to cover all the main aspects of Christ's saving work gives us at least a hint of something which always distinguishes the new man in Christ no matter into what situation he may come. It will be my purpose to develop and illustrate that hint as we go on, but meanwhile I state it summarily in this form: it is the mark of the new man in Christ that he is continually thrust into the midst of stresses and tensions and yet at the same time is given peace and victory in face of them. He is not, by virtue of being saved, exempted from, called out of, the conflicts and oppositions of man's historical existence. On the contrary, he is required to remain in the midst of them; indeed, it is often part of the work of Christ to make him more acutely aware of them than he could ever otherwise be, and even to add to them. But he *is* given victory and peace in relation to them; in a deep and distinctive way he is reconciled to them, even while paradoxically he is called strenuously to wrestle with them. He is reconciled to them because he is reconciled to *God* through Christ; his is 'an inward peace subsisting at the heart of endless agitation'. The Apostle Paul has vividly expressed this paradoxical quality of the Christian life: 'we are afflicted in every way, but not crushed; perplexed, but not driven to despair; persecuted, but not forsaken; struck down, but not destroyed'. And again: 'as unknown and yet well known; as dying, and behold we live; as punished,[4] yet not killed; as sorrowful, yet always rejoicing; as poor, yet making many rich; as having nothing, and yet possessing all things'.[5] It is only necessary to make this perhaps somewhat obvious point because the impulse to think of salvation as, almost by definition, bringing release or exemption from the pressures, conflicts and tensions of life, or at least a considerable reduction of them—certainly not adding to them— is very strong and persistent in the human spirit. Yet nothing could be more remote from the New Testament understanding of salvation and reconciliation with God.

(2)

Seeking, then, to explore and expound our Lord's saving work as Reconciler, I propose to make use of the schema, more or less traditional in Protestant theology, of the three so-called 'offices' of Christ, the *munus triplex*— his office as prophet, as priest, as king. I have always felt that these three ancient and familiar symbols constitute a very useful framework or ground-plan for any who would wish to understand and set forth in the fullest way what Christ can and does do savingly for a man. Of course, they are no more than symbols and have to be used

[4] Better translated 'disciplined'.
[5] 2 *Corinthians* 4, 8–9; 6, 9–10 (R.S.V.). Cf. *Romans* 8, 36–37.

circumspectly, care being taken not to confuse metaphorical with literal statements; but so used, they can help us to do fuller justice to what St Paul calls 'the immeasurable riches of God's grace towards us in Christ Jesus'.[6] Theologians have pointed out the dangers and pitfalls which beset the use of the symbols, and some have counselled dropping them altogether.[7] It is said that they are much too figurative, too elastic and popular, to serve careful theological reflection; that each theologian tends to put merely his own and not always consistent meaning into them; that there is the ever-present danger of the three offices getting split off from one another or set over against one another, so that the massive unity of Christ's person and saving work is destroyed. Such comments and warnings are no doubt salutary, but I do not see that they need forbid us the use of the schema altogether. *Prima facie* the three offices do seem to be related to three central and permanent needs of the human spirit which must in some way be met if a man is to be saved, the need for truth, the need for forgiveness, the need for an absolute to rule and to empower, and that being so the schema need not be a merely traditional and lifeless formula artificially and restrictively imposed on the living reality of the Christian saving revelation and faith, but rather one which can be continually related to and vitalized by it. In any case, the proof of the theological pudding is in the eating, if one may so put it; if we find the schema of the three offices a help in preparing and serving the pudding, there seems no good reason why we should not make use of it.

---

[6] *Ephesians* 2, 7.
[7] E.g. A. B. Macaulay, *The Death of Jesus* (London, Hodder & Stoughton, 1938), pp. 55 ff.

We may begin from a line of thought which runs through Ritschl's lengthy treatment of the offices of Christ.[8] Ritschl, to be sure, has been in recent years under something of a cloud in theological circles, but it is still possible to learn something, and even a good deal, from his profound and penetrating discussion of theological questions. Ritschl reacted from the treatment of the saving work of Christ in earlier Protestant dogmatics, particularly as set forth under the schema of the three offices, broadly on the ground that that work tended to be thought of altogether apart from the personal consciousness and inner life of the Redeemer in the days of his flesh. These fell almost completely into the background. The tendency was to think of him primarily as the second Person of the Trinity who in the inscrutable wisdom of the Godhead was appointed to carry through a plan or programme for the salvation of mankind; in accordance with this his saving work was not thought of as related to and springing from a deep inward transaction of his own human personal life; it was not envisaged as both flowing from and contributing to his own profound and perfect fellowship with his heavenly Father to whom he looked up in complete obedience and trust. Rather what he did 'for us men and our salvation' he did officially, *ex officio*, merely functionally, just as a man—to compare small things with great—when required might fulfil the office or function of juryman without it entering significantly into his personal life as a man, its interests and plans and hopes and destiny. Thus, what was termed Christ's prophetic office tended to be thought of and expounded as being primarily the

---

[8] A. Ritschl, *The Christian Doctrine of Justification and Reconciliation*, Eng. tr. by H. R. Mackintosh and A. B. Macaulay (Edinburgh, T. & T. Clark, 1900), III, Ch. 6.

B

declaration of truth which he did not need to learn for himself in a human mode of learning at all; it was not truth wrought out and embodied in, mediated through, 'proved on the pulses' (to use Keats' famous phrase), of a personal, historical life, but rather truth magisterially possessed and announced; its authority was not that of a piercing moral and spiritual splendour which like the sun is discerned by its own light, but rather that of a divine oracle not to be questioned. Similarly, his priestly office tended to be conceived in a way even more detached from his inner, personal life, from his own strenuous submission of himself to God's rule in his life, his own giving of himself in unutterable love to mankind. His death on the Cross was something which had to be undergone in order to exempt men from the otherwise inevitable consequences of their sin; it was a role 'officially' assumed for a purpose laid down by the rigour of the divine justice and by the programme or plan of salvation which that justice prescribed. A parallel line of thought was followed in respect of his kingly office. The scope of this was indeed expressly limited by some theologians to his so-called 'state of exaltation' (*status exaltationis*) with the result that here also his earthly personal life (the so-called *status exinantionis*) was thrust completely into the background.

Ritschl, as I have said, reacted from this, and rightly so. Broadly, his thought, if I may paraphrastically summarize it, was that we must not be misled by the concept of 'office', even if we find it otherwise convenient to use; and the way to avoid this is not to make it the primary and fundamental concept. Rather we should always think and speak primarily of Christ's *vocation* and make that regulative of all else. The force of this term 'vocation' for Ritschl as a protection against the errors indicated is to be seen in the definition he gave of it. By a vocation in ordinary life, he says in his somewhat ponderous Teutonic manner, we mean work 'in the regular pursuit of which the individual realizes at once his own self-end and the common ultimate end of human society'.[9] Transferring this, *mutatis mutandis*, to the work of Christ, the word 'vocation' signifies and emphasizes that what he accomplished for us men and our salvation had the profoundest possible significance for his own life and being as a historic, human person.[10] Back of, more fundamental than, the 'offices', if we still care to use that scheme of symbols, is the person, the word 'person' being here used, not to signify, as it tended to do in the older dogmatics, the more or less abstract theological concept of the second Person of the Trinity, but the concrete personal life of the Saviour as lived in the midst of human historical existence. Ritschl contended that by thus grounding the three offices in the *one* vocation of Christ we are not only enabled to keep our thought of the work of Christ closely related to his person in the way just indicated but are also prevented from losing sight of the unity of the three offices with one another even though we have in a measure to separate them from one another for the purposes of exposition.

At this point we may leave Ritschl, taking from him only this central concept of 'vocation'. How shall we describe and define the vocation of Christ? The answer to this has already been indicated. We describe and define it as that of reconciliation, that of the Reconciler. Christ's vocation is to be the source and sustainer in men and

[9] Op. cit., p. 445.
[10] 'What Jesus actually was and accomplished, that he is in the first place for himself.' (Op. cit., p. 442.)

women of the life which is fully reconciled to God. Into this vocation his three offices of prophet, priest and king enter indispensably and inseparably, and by it they are kept together in unity with one another; they constitute the seamless robe of his *one* inclusive vocation as our Reconciler and our Reconciliation. This unity of the three offices under the one vocation and the importance of always bearing it in mind will, I hope, become apparent as we treat of them separately in the remaining lectures. The point, however, that I want now to make arises from the fundamental meaning of the term 'vocation' as applied to our Lord's saving work; it is that the reconciliation which he accomplishes for us and in us he first had in and for himself in the fulness and richness of his own personal life; moreover he had it in a form determined by the fact that his vocation was to accomplish this work for us. These two things are connected together: he is able to accomplish it in us and for us precisely because he himself first had it in his own personal life, and also because he had it in the form determined by his vocation to accomplish it in us and for us. In short, Christ is able to be our Reconciliation, our Reconciler, because he is in his own person supremely, fully, *par excellence*, the reconciled man.

In the light of this it is clear where we must look for the answer to the questions with which we started: what does it mean to be a reconciled man, reconciled through Christ? what are the distinctive characteristics of such a man? We must look for it in the first instance in the person of Christ himself, the perfectly reconciled one, as he meets us in the Gospels. But also, because he is the perfectly reconciled one not apart from, but only in and through, his unique vocation and work of reconciliation, we must not

in this matter isolate the Gospels from the remainder of
the New Testament. In the latter we are able to observe
Christ's work of reconciliation being actually accomplished
in the lives of men through the immediate, recreative
impact upon them of his mind and spirit, his teaching and
life and death and resurrection. The New Testament as a
whole, in other words, is and always must be our primary
source, beginning indeed with the Gospels and him who
encounters us there, but at the same time illumining and
confirming and interpreting what we find there by what
we can observe Christ actually accomplishing in the lives
of men as this is exhibited to us in the Acts and the
Epistles. We discern the nature of the reconciled life as set
forth in the portrait of Christ in the Gospels more clearly
and surely by means of the reconciliation which we can
see him accomplishing in the lives of men as set forth in
the remainder of the New Testament; and we discern the
nature of the reconciled life as set forth in the remainder of
the New Testament more clearly and surely by means
of the reconciled life as set forth in Christ in the Gospels.

By thus holding Gospels and Epistles together in reciprocal interplay with one another we are not only enabled
to keep Christ's historic person as the perfectly reconciled
one and the work of reconciliation he effects in and for men
in that unity with one another which is implied by the
concept of vocation, but are also given part of the answer
to the problem which has been raised, or at least given a
new basis and emphasis, by the work of form-criticism on
the Gospel records. It is now, of course, generally recognized that the material presented to us in the Gospels has
been shaped to a not negligible degree by the faith and
practice of the early Christian community, especially by
its catechetical, preaching and liturgical needs. But the

inference sometimes drawn from this that therefore we cannot really encounter and know the real, historic Christ in the pages of the Gospels, the real, historic Christ being hidden from us by the interpretative transformations of the community, is highly questionable if only for the reason indicated in what I have just been saying, namely, that it makes an improper cleavage between the historic person of Christ and the work of reconciliation he accomplishes in the lives of men. The person of Christ is in part revealed by what he thus accomplishes, and if the acts and words and character of Christ as set forth in the Gospels have in some measure been shaped by the faith and experience of the infant Church, they are not falsified thereby, for he himself by the impact of those acts and words and character created and called forth that faith and experience. Interpretation is not falsification, particularly if the principles on which the interpretation is made are themselves creatively given and sustained by what is being interpreted.

(3)

We turn then to the Gospels to see what we can gather from them in answer to the question what it means to be a reconciled man. I suggest that we can discern four elements in, characteristics of, the distinctively Christian reconciled life, the life, that is, which is shaped by Christ who is himself the perfectly reconciled man, the life which bears his distinctive stamp and style.

First, to be reconciled to God is to be reconciled to Him in respect of sin. We shall consider this more fully in the third lecture; meanwhile it is sufficient for our purpose to say that it means two things which *prima facie* seem paradoxically opposed to one another; yet the distinctive heart and essence of Christ's reconciling work in this matter of sin resides in the paradox. On the one hand, the reconciled man consciously stands in God's living and holy presence—*really* stands there—and so standing genuinely, humbly and penitently acknowledges his sin and sinfulness. I say *really* stands there because it is possible for a man to suppose that he is standing there in the sense that is here intended when he is not, and so to be penitent, or appear to be so both to himself and to others, in a way that is shallow and self-deceived. The reconciled man has a genuine vision of himself as he really is in the sight of God as He really is. He is now in God's real world, the world of 'God's truth', and so is no longer in the world of illusion about himself and his relation to God, about the nature and extent and culpability of his sinful condition. On the other hand, because and only because he thus stands humbly penitent in God's presence, the burden and anxiety of remorse and guilt, of unavailing self-reproach and self-despising and consequent attempts continually to excuse and justify himself, and all that this means of inward conflict and strain, so far from being intensified beyond bearing as one might expect it to be, are taken away. Paradoxical as it sounds, it is given to the reconciled man in the very act of acknowledging and repudiating his sin to be somehow content to be a sinner in God's presence, to stand before God just as he is, *sin and all*, and to be accepted of Him not because he can point to at least some merit to be set on the other side of the account, not because he can urge a claim or put forward extenuating or compensatory excuses and considerations, but simply and wholly and solely because of God's gracious mercy and pardon. Here we may observe that aspect of reconciliation to which reference was made earlier,[11] namely, that tensions and oppositions remain in and through the very process of their being continually overcome. The reconciled man is at peace about his sin in the presence of God, yet precisely because it is in the presence of God that he stands he does not and cannot cease to be deeply and poignantly conscious of it even while at peace about it.

This first and most fundamental aspect of what we may gather from the Gospels of what it means to be a reconciled man does not there find expression, it is hardly necessary to say, in so many terms, least of all in the sort of abstract terms I have just been using: but it is there in a way that is the more impressive for being implicit and presented to us in living characters and concrete instances. It seems quite evident that deep and central in our Lord's view of man's relation to God is the thought that a man must, if he is to enter into a new life, come to see himself and continue to see himself as he really is in God's presence; yet precisely because it *is* in God's presence that he sees this he is to be at peace about it, *God being what He is*. The most moving expression of this, of course, is in the parable of the prodigal. This man, it is said, 'comes to himself', or, as the New English Bible renders it, 'comes to his senses'; comes out of the false world of folly and self-deception into the real world; projects himself and his manner of life back into the home he had left and sees them as they really are in the light of that context. He hugs no more illusions about himself, is stripped of every kind of posturing and excuse-making and self-justification. So he returns to his father 'just as he is', with the filth and mire of the pig-sties still upon him, putting up no claim and making no plea except to go where he

[11] See above, p. 4.

has shown he belongs—among the hired hands! 'Make me as one of the hired servants; I am not fit to be called thy son'—I see and accept the truth that I am a 'bad lot'. And in that frame of mind he is received back, unconditionally, unreservedly, joyously—as a son.[12]

Then there is the brief and pregnant parable of the pharisee and the publican, with which may be taken the startling logion that tax-gatherers and prostitutes go into the Kingdom of God before the 'chief priests and elders'.[13] In the parable the publican stands humbly in the presence of God, sees himself as he is in that searching light; he bows his head and accepts the truth, seeking no other refuge than God's pardoning mercy; and instantly he is on a new footing with God. Thus humbling himself he is at once forgiven and exalted, 'goes down justified'. Again, there is the parable of the labourers in the vineyard: it is clearly the underlying presupposition of this, whatever may be taken to be its main import, that no man can stand in the presence of God without finding himself confronted with a generosity so overflowing that any thought of earning or deserving or presenting a claim is completely out of place, a generosity which both reveals and repudiates the lack of such generosity, the lovelessness, which is characteristic of men.[14] Or again, the incident in the Pharisee's house of the woman who was a sinner and washed Christ's feet with her tears and wiped them with the hairs of her head.[15] Some, perhaps, will feel some difficulty in accepting the story just as it stands; a case can be made for the view that it was put together and even in some degree imaginatively elaborated and shaped, in the interests of preaching, from a simpler incident or

[12] *Luke* 15, 17 ff.
[13] *Luke* 18, 9 ff.; *Matthew* 21, 31.
[14] *Matthew* 20, 1 ff.
[15] *Luke* 7, 36 ff.

incidents or some parable spoken by Christ on another occasion. But even so, it surely can hardly be questioned that in its essential meaning it bears the distinctive stamp of Christ's unique person and teaching, a meaning which neither the first disciples nor the early preachers of the *kerugma* could have invented. And does it not vividly express and illustrate this aspect of reconciliation of which we are here speaking? In the parable which Christ is represented as telling to Simon the Pharisee the central emphasis is on the fact that the two debtors had nothing whatever wherewith to discharge the debt and yet were forgiven it, the forgiveness evoking in them a response of grateful love. And in applying the parable to the woman our Lord is manifestly discerning in her extravagant action that deep and true penitence which God meets instantly with forgiveness and with the setting of her in a new relation to Himself of reconciliation and peace. 'And he said to the woman, thy sins are forgiven, thy faith hath saved thee, go in peace.'

We may digress for a little here to note that this moving story has perhaps some bearing on a question which presents itself in connection with the line of thought we have been pursuing. Our thought has been that Christ fulfils his vocation as the Reconciler, as the source of our reconciliation and peace, by virtue of the fact that he is himself the perfectly reconciled one; it is for this reason, we have said, that we look first to him to answer the question what it means to be a new, reconciled man. But, it may be asked, how can this be so in regard to this aspect of the reconciled life of which we are here speaking, namely, that the sinner is reconciled to God in respect of his sinfulness through penitence and the divine forgiveness which meets it? For Christ, we believe, was without sin; how then can he be in himself the perfectly reconciled one in respect to sin and its forgiveness? That Christ, in his pure and perfect goodness, should have had an utterly clear vision of God and of God's relation to sinful men denied to the latter because of their sinfulness and the blindness it inevitably brings, is wholly comprehensible—'blessed are the pure in heart, for they shall see God'—and is indeed a truth on which the Christian faith in him as the Way, the Truth and the Life ultimately rests. But that he should have known in his own personal life the divine forgiveness which instantly meets true and deep penitence, so that in this regard he can in any proper or realistic sense be said to be in himself the perfectly reconciled one seems to be excluded by the concept of sinless perfection itself. Perhaps we may go some way towards an answer to this question by giving a right positive content to what is otherwise apt to be a much too negative idea of sinlessness, a content which we derive from Christ himself. That right positive content is his perfect love, or *agapé*, grounded in his unclouded fellowship with and vision of God. Christ is sinless, not because of a negative avoidance of, or abstention from, this or that objectionable or prohibited behaviour, but because of a mighty, positive, utterly selfless love to men such as we in our sinful alienation from God and consequent alienation and separation from one another can hardly comprehend, much less share. Yet this I think we can comprehend: such love, because it is utterly pure and selfless, has within it a power of imaginative self-identification, of deeply felt and understanding 'empathy' (to use what seems to be becoming a somewhat cliché and over-used term), with and towards another human person and what is taking place in his mind and spirit. The place of such imaginative, 'empathetic' self-identification in agapeistic love has never perhaps been adequately emphasized and explored.[16] For me it is not possible to read the story of this sinful penitent woman and of Jesus' relation to her without receiving the impression that he was somehow right inside her situation and her spirit with her, was, in a very real sense, 'weeping with her',[17] in her lack of what he himself so fully and richly enjoyed through his fellowship with God, and in her poignantly penitent consciousness of that lack to which through her sin and her encounter with him she had now come. A like 'empathy' we may perhaps discern behind the parable of the prodigal, for otherwise it is difficult to understand how our Lord could have penetrated so unerringly to the 'coming to himself' of such a wastrel. 'Make me as one of thy hired servants'—the words ring true; yet Christ could never have known their truth through any penitent return of his own from the 'far country' and 'riotous living'. Arthur Shearly Cripps, in his poem 'The Death of Saint Francis', has pictured in moving words such 'empathetic' self-identification of Christlike love:

> I knew in blissful anguish what it means
> To be a part of Christ, and feel as mine
> The dark distresses of my brother limbs,
> To feel it bodily and simply true,
> To feel as mine the starving of his poor,
> To feel as mine the shadow of curse on all,
> Hard words, hard looks and savage misery,
> And struggling deaths, unpitied and unwept.
> To feel rich brothers' sad satieties,
> The weary manner of their lives and deaths,
> That want in love, and lacking love lack all.

[16] Cf. T. E. Jessop, *The Christian Morality* (London, The Epworth Press, 1960), p. 77.

[17] *Romans* 12, 15.

May we not think that some such self-identification with the penitence of the awakened sinner entered into our Lord's consciousness, that in some real and not merely sentimental way he 'felt it as his', felt it indeed in a deeper way because of his infinitely clearer perception of the sinfulness of sin and all that is at stake in it both for the sinner and for God? And may we not think that to such 'empathetic' penitence it was given to apprehend, not under the form of the general theological truth that God forgives, but livingly, here and now, 'on his own pulses', in relation to the concrete particularity of this penitent man or woman, the reality and wonder of the infinite mercy of God, that infinite mercy which goes forth instantly to meet the penitent man, to encompass him, to draw him back into the restored circle of fellowship, reconciled? And may we not think that it was these things taken together—his own deep sense of the sinfulness of sin, his entering into the penitence of the sinner 'feeling it as his own', his own living awareness of the divine pardon going forth to meet such penitence—which imparted to his words 'thy sins are forgiven thee' their unique power to convince and to give peace to those to whom he spoke them?[18]

(4)

The *second* element in the Christian reconciled life which we can learn from the life, teaching and person of Christ as these come before us in the Gospels is this: to be

[18] Perhaps it should be pointed out that I am not here making use of the difficult and questionable concept of 'vicarious penitence', a penitence, that is to say, which in some fashion can act as a *substitute* for the sinner's own penitence. On the contrary, in what has been said the sinner's own penitence is obviously presupposed. But see below, pp. 68 ff.

reconciled to God means to be reconciled to all His requirements of us.

No one certainly has ever set before men a more lofty and austere ideal of character and conduct than Christ, both by his explicit teaching and by the whole content and quality of his life. There are negative precepts, or precepts of negative import, of the most rigorous kind demanding the completest cleansing of innermost motive and the completest surrender of outward advantage. And there are positive standards and ideals so high that many have seriously questioned whether they are within the range of what is possible for men.[19] On the other hand, nothing could be more manifestly false to the mind of Christ and to the new style of life to which he called men than to suppose that he did no more than impose an ethic more exacting than any before or since. That he would have emphatically repudiated the notion that he was merely laying fresh burdens on men's already overburdened consciences is shown by the note of joyous emancipation with which he proclaims his message,[20] and by his criticism of Pharisaic religion, a criticism which finds moving and memorable expression in the words 'Come unto me, all ye that labour and are heavy laden, and I will give you rest. Take my yoke upon you, and learn of me . . . for my yoke is easy and my burden is light.'[21] The requirements of God, in other words, do not flow from a hard, distant and exacting righteousness which does no more than impose commands and duties and

[19] E.g. *Matthew* 5, 29–30; *Luke* 14, 26; *Mark* 10, 23–27; etc.

[20] *Mark* 2, 19; *Luke* 4, 18; 15, 6, 9, 23 f.

[21] *Matthew* 11, 28 ff. Even if, in view of echoes and parallels elsewhere, there may be some reason to doubt whether these are the exact words of Jesus, there can be no question that they marvellously embody his unique mind and spirit and his sense of his unique vocation.

takes note of disobediences with an inexorably penalizing eye, and which therefore a man had better obey for fear of consequences or, at best, out of hope of reward. The tendency towards such a legalistic, duty religion was undoubtedly present in Pharisaic Judaism—indeed it is powerfully at work in one form or another in every human heart—and it is clearly a dominant purpose in the mind of Christ to lift men right out of such religion into a new world of reconciliation to God wherein the doing of His will is no longer a drudgery of reluctant and uninspired compliance sustained only by the thought of reward, but the soul's veritable meat and drink.[22] Yet it is to be noted that he also spoke of a man 'taking up his cross'. Reconciliation to God's requirements is certainly not presented to us in the Gospels as a way of life from which strenuousness, the necessity to hold oneself to the doing of God's will in the teeth of other incentives, motives and desires, is excluded. This is evident from Christ's own experience. He was himself subject to temptation. 'Ye are they,' he said to his disciples, 'who have continued with me in my temptations.' 'I have a baptism to be baptized with, and how I am straitened until it be accomplished.' And the tautness of his will in face of such temptation is shown by the vehemence of his rebuke to Peter when the latter sought to persuade him not to tread the way of the Cross: 'Get thee behind me, Satan.'[23] Yet, even so, it is manifest that this strenuous loyalty to the will of God is a very different thing from action out of no more than a sense of duty with perhaps an eye on subsequent rewards or penalties. The latter cannot properly be called reconcilia-

[22] 'It is meat and drink for me to do the will of him that sent me' (*John* 4, 34, N.E.B.).
[23] *Matthew* 4, 1 ff.; 16, 23; *Luke* 12, 50; 22, 28.

tion at all: the former issues in an obedience and self-commitment which is real reconciliation, as when Christ prayed in the garden, though the sweat fell from him we are told as blood, 'Father, if thou be willing, remove this cup from me: nevertheless not my will, but thine, be done.'[24] The use of the word 'Father' in this prayer points the contrast. In all this we discern once again the characteristic quality of Christian reconciliation, namely, that tensions and oppositions are not removed or reduced; they persist in and through the very overcoming of them in victory and peace.

(5)

The *third* element in the reconciled life which we learn from the Gospels is: to be reconciled to God is to be reconciled to all His appointments. No matter what life may bring, the reconciled man is enabled to accept it, including even the bitterest disappointment, frustration and suffering, as from the hand of God and to be at peace. He has been—to use St Paul's phrase—'initiated into the secret', the secret, 'in whatsoever state he is, therewith to be content', the secret of acceptance.[25] Neither rebellion and resentment nor a dull, despairing acquiescence and resignation find place in his spirit. He knows in his own being and life the truth of the words which Katharine Mansfield wrote in the midst of the frustration and suffering of her early fatal illness: 'everything that one really accepts undergoes a change'.

This is so manifestly distinctive of the mind of Christ that it hardly needs dwelling on. There is the frequent witness of his teaching: the exhortations not to fear or be

---

[24] *Luke* 22, 42.   [25] *Philippians* 4, 11 ff.

anxious; the rebukes to his disciples for their unbelief and lack of faith—'O ye little-faiths!' sounds on his lips almost like a sorrowful nickname for them; the very revealing word 'which of you by being anxious can add one cubit to his stature?' as though to say 'why not humbly accept God's appointment of your height and physique, whatever these may be?'—a rebuke to that most widespread and destructive manifestation of the unreconciled life, the so-called 'inferiority complex'; the warnings against worrying about the future and seeking to make provision for it instead of living a day at a time in the doing of God's will, and so on.[26] Along with the teaching and shining through it there is the even more powerful witness of his own life as it unfolds amidst the conditions, the pressures and challenges and needs, of contemporary human existence and mounts to its climax in the Cross. Everything is lifted into the context of the love and wisdom and power of the Father. 'With God all things are possible.' 'Your Father knoweth what things ye have need of, before ye ask him.'[27] Even the fugitive grasses and flowers of the field are clothed by God, and a sparrow falling in fluttering distress to the ground is in the grasp of the knowledge and will of God who numbers even the very hairs of men's heads.[28] He sleeps in the midst of the storm on the lake, and is quiet and self-possessed in the presence of a raving imbecile, imparting to him, it would appear, something of the peace of his own spirit.[29] His life-story is one of increasing disappointment and frustration culminating in his Passion; yet never is he dispossessed of his essential victory and peace. All is accepted as from the hand of God; yet

[26] *Matthew* 6, 25 ff.; 8, 26 ff.; 14, 31; 16, 8; 6, 11.
[27] *Matthew* 19, 26; 6, 8. [28] *Matthew* 6, 30; 10, 29 f.
[29] *Mark* 4, 37; *Luke* 8, 26 ff.

c

this, be it noted once again, in no smooth and easy way
and certainly in no mood of merely stoical resignation. On
the contrary, he keeps his mind clear to the vision of God
and undefeated by anxiety and fear by a strenuousness of
spirit of which we are given glimpses in his frequent with-
drawal to pray,[30] and of which we have more than a
glimpse in the agony in the Garden and in the cry of dereliction from the Cross. Even in that dreadful darkness his
spirit was laying hold of God and coming to rest in His
overshadowing love and providence. The cry was addressed to his Father, and was followed a little later by a
final prayer of self-commitment and peace: 'Father, into
thy hands I commend my spirit.'[31]

Here again we meet the paradox of Christian reconciliation already referred to, namely, that tension and conflict
remain even in the continuous overcoming of them.

(6)

Fourth, we learn from the Gospels that to be reconciled
to God means to be reconciled to one's fellow-men in a
new kind of personal relationship. Here again is something so central and fundamental in our Lord's teaching
and outlook that it hardly requires exposition and exemplification. It meets us explicitly or implicitly on almost
every page of the Gospels. It is the most obvious, the most
challenging, and even to an unsympathetic and unbeliev-
ing mind perhaps the most distinctive, typical and ad-
mirable characteristic of a specifically 'Christ-style' of life.
This new relation to persons we have no single word to
describe except the word 'love', but unhappily this is such

[30] *Matthew* 14, 23; *Mark* 1, 35; 6, 46; *Luke* 6, 12; 9, 28 ff.; 5, 16.
[31] *Luke* 22, 40 ff.; 23, 46; *Matthew* 27, 46. See also below, p. 77.

an ambiguous and multivalent word, so exhausted by continuous misuse, that it is practically worthless for the purpose; we have little option, therefore, but to fall back upon a circular definition and say that by 'love' here we mean precisely that sort of relation to persons taught and exemplified by Christ himself. It is best indicated, as is now generally recognized, by the distinctive New Testament usage of the term *agapé*: *agapé* is the love and concern which go out to a human person for no other reason than that he is a human person, than that he is 'there', not because he is such and such, not because he has agreeable and attractive qualities of one sort or another or is likely to bestow benefits in return. It is a going forth to the other man in a strong and undeviating desire for, and will to, fellowship (another word worn flat and thin with use, but we have no other) with him; it is thus deeply imbued in its essential nature with the spirit and intention of reconciliation no matter what barriers and obstacles he may set up. There are few things which our Lord insisted on more often than that it is impossible to be in a right and reconciled relation to God and *not* be in this new attitude and relation to other persons, and this very particularly in those situations in which natural feelings, if given their rein, lead inevitably to and perpetuate estrangement and enmity.[32] This however must be added, though it ought not really to be necessary to do so: it is clear that to be in this new relation to men did not mean for Christ in the least degree being a mildly inoffensive person who bleats pathetically or gushes effusively about 'loving one another'; rather it is to be an active reconciler, one who faces and accepts the demands of God's righteousness both upon himself and upon the other man, and that is a costing

[32] *Matthew* 5, 23 f.; 5, 43 f.; 6, 14 f.; 18, 21 f, 35; *Mark* 11, 25 f.

business requiring for its discharge that a man should enter
into those other aspects of reconciliation to God of which
we have been speaking—reconciliation to Him in respect
of one's sin, in respect of His requirements, in respect of
His appointments. 'Blessed are the peacemakers, for they
shall be called the children of God';[33] yet, be it noted, it
is of peace*making* that Christ here speaks and that is
an active verb; it is not a matter, as Oman has said, of
being merely peaceable.[34] The very next beatitude runs
'Blessed are ye when men shall revile you, and persecute
you'. Peacemaking of this high order may involve you in
reviling and persecution, yet even so you are still blessed,
still a man deeply reconciled to God. Once again we
observe how conflict and opposition persist through the
new, reconciled life.

(7)

We have, then, these four aspects of, elements in, the
picture of the reconciled life which is given us in the
Gospel records of our Lord's life and teaching: reconciliation to God in respect of sin—forgiveness; reconciliation
to God in respect of His requirements—obedience;
reconciliation to God in respect of His appointments—
trust; reconciliation to God in respect of a new relation to
other persons—brotherly love which goes out to all men,
agapé. We must now note, in harmony with what was
said earlier, that the same picture comes to us through
the other writings of the New Testament also, giving
them an essential unity with the Gospels and with one

[33] *Matthew* 5, 9.
[34] J. W. Oman, *Grace and Personality*, Collins Fontana edition, p. 96; first
published by Cambridge, The University Press. My indebtedness to the
work will be apparent.

another in spite of a variety of modes of expression. The New Testament writers are all humble, penitent and forgiven men in whom Christ has wrought his strange, paradoxical work of making them deeply disturbed about their sinfulness and yet setting their hearts at peace about it. And they lay down the highest ideals of character and conduct without any apology for asking so much or the least hint that such ideals are too exalted for the new man in Christ to achieve. 'Put on', writes the Apostle, 'mercifulness, kindness, humbleness of mind'—all the virtues of Christ—almost as though it were as easy as putting on your hat! And everywhere the new man is presented as possessing the secret of victory and peace in the midst of every trial and affliction, every limitation and frustration, of human existence, and above all every suffering which arises, and indeed must arise, out of the life of Christian discipleship itself. Finally, all these men write out of the heart of the Christian community, the new fellowship of persons which is constituted by the entirely transformed relation of its members to one another through their common relation to Christ.[35]

(8)

We must now turn for a little to another fundamental aspect of the picture of the saved and reconciled man which meets us in the Gospels. We must do this not only because it is of the highest importance in itself but also because it has a bearing on our Lord's sense of his own unique vocation and is related to some things we shall want to discuss later, particularly in connection with his kingly office.

[35] See, *inter alia*, *Romans* 5, 1–11; 8, 35–37; 12, 14–21; *Colossians* 3, 10–15.

In what has been said so far there has been no mention of a conception which is obviously central and dominant in the Gospels—the conception of the Kingdom of God. To any one coming to the Gospels with a fresh mind the obvious short answer to the question what a man needs to be saved into, 'reconciled into' if one may use such a phrase, would be 'the Kingdom of God'. No phrase occurs more frequently, indeed as frequently, on the lips of Christ. Clearly, therefore, an exposition of what it means to be a saved and reconciled man according to the Gospels is seriously incomplete without some consideration of how the thought of the Kingdom enters in.

Perhaps we may best approach this by taking note of two aspects of the mind and teaching of our Lord which at first sight appear to be incongruous with one another. On the one hand, he appears not infrequently to speak of the Kingdom of God as lying in the future, not a far distant and vaguely promissory future but one so imminent that it constitutes an immediate and overhanging crisis for men. This impending, formidable event is somehow connected with his own person and advent into history, but when it comes it will in some fashion be the conclusion and consummation of history and its long travail in the final overthrow of evil and the fully realized victory and reign of God. The Kingdom is a transhistorical, transmundane reality to be brought about only by the finger of God's power. In short—to use a technical term—Christ's thought of the Kingdom is apocalyptic. On the other hand, he speaks of the Kingdom not as merely future but as a present fact here and now powerfully operative amongst men, and this supremely and uniquely so through himself and through his own ministry of healing and teaching and challenge. He summons men to recognize this fact, to respond to it *now* in a critical and decisive act of repentance and self-commitment, and thus to enter *now* through discipleship to himself into their true 'blessedness'. Conformably with this there is plainly manifest in his whole being—and life that 'blessedness' of which we have just spoken—a poise, a breadth, a quiet-mindedness (albeit combined with strenuous energy and decision), a concern for and a willingness to give himself to ordinary men and women and their needs, a love for the birds, the flowers and the children, an eye for the familiar, commonplace, domestic things, activities and relations of everyday human life, which is far removed from the often fanatical and overheated apocalypticism of the time. His is the 'meekness' which he himself said inherits *the earth*. In short, he provides impressive exemplification of the reconciled life which we have been describing.[36]

Different ways of resolving, or at least reducing, this *prima facie* contrariety have been at various times proposed. Some have sought to explain away, or at least to minimize and tone down, the second of the two aspects; taken to its extreme, this leaves us with a picture of Christ as little more than a charming and amiable Galilean preacher, the 'gentle Jesus meek and mild' of the children's hymn. Others have sought to put all the emphasis on this second aspect, and this taken to its extreme leaves us with a picture of Christ as little more than a tense, whirlwind herald of 'last things' summoning men to live as those who are in

[36] A great deal of Gospel material has, of course, been condensed in this paragraph, much of it raising difficult questions of exegesis. I forbear, therefore, from providing detailed documentation. But of the general truth of the picture given of the two contrasting aspects of Christ's life and teaching there can hardly be question. The reader may perhaps be referred to C. H. Dodd's *The Parables of the Kingdom* (London, James Nisbet & Co. Ltd, 1935), Ch. 2; and G. Bornkamm's *Jesus of Nazareth* (London, Hodder & Stoughton, 1960), p. 90.

a world shortly to be annulled and who themselves are to be caught up in the divine kingdom thus brought to pass. Others, again, have sought to make room for both aspects by separating them chronologically from one another: to the earlier period of his ministry belongs predominantly that side of his temper and teaching which is large, sunny, tender, peaceful; to the latter belongs the apocalyptic side, the urgency of which culminates in a needless immolation of himself on the Cross through misguided notions of himself as the Messiah. In its extreme expression this view does not shrink from ascribing the transition from the one period to the other to at least a partial derangement of his mind.

We cannot be satisfied with any of these three views. The first two are wrong in emphasizing one of the two aspects at the expense of the other; both aspects are indubitably and equally present in the Gospel portrait of Christ. The third is right in holding to both aspects but wrong in separating them from one another and above all in supposing that the transition from the one to the other took place through some alienation of mind; the integrity of the mind of Christ must surely be axiomatic in all our interpretation of the Gospels. Adhering to this we must maintain, and seek to discern, that the two aspects are in closest organic unity with one another. Surely it is not difficult to discern this, to discern that there is a profound inward connection between the life of 'reconciliation' which our Lord lived right in the midst of this present world and his faith concerning his Father's Kingdom and its coming, the faith, that is, in a divine rule which while it is livingly present and active in this world nevertheless transcends this world in its final consummation, such final consummation when it comes (as come it must and at any time may) being brought to pass by God's own will and decision. Christ's is the peace and the power, the quiet-mindedness and yet also the strenuousness, of the life here and now in this present world fully reconciled to God precisely because his is the unclouded awareness that the here and now of this present world lies wholly within the grasp of a sovereign, divine purpose, an all-encompassing wisdom and love, which alike in its scope and in the way of its final victory transcends this present world altogether.

(9)

This brings us to a further central and fundamental element in our Lord's thought of the Kingdom, one which we have more than once hinted at already. I have just spoken of his 'uniquely unclouded awareness' of the presence and purpose of God in the world. The phrase is perhaps not a very happy one: 'unclouded awareness' seems too flat and jejune to convey the 'uniqueness', the depth and power, of his personal life and its immeasurable effects in the lives and destiny of men and in the unfolding of history. It corrects this impression to note that the Gospel records show that his 'awareness' of God was grounded in and sustained by a profound sense of *his own unique vocation* in relation to the Kingdom, in the counsels of God and the working out of His purpose with men. It is plain from the records that his whole being and life were possessed and controlled by the conviction that in himself the Kingdom, God's saving rule and purpose in the world, had come into effective operation in a new, once-for-all way, that his own advent into history was the inception of a great divine saving, self-revealing action towards men which would be completed and consummated beyond history in the full and final establishment of the Kingdom. In accordance with this he appears to think of his own person as of central, decisive, indispensable importance in the 'saving' of men, the bringing of them into the 'Kingdom', into the new life of reconciliation with God of which we have been treating in this lecture. The fulfilment of his vocation is bound up with men's relation to himself, with their readiness to commit themselves without reservation to his discipleship.

If we take together as elements in a single picture the regal way in which he called men to forsake all and at any cost to follow him;[37] the sovereign attitude he adopted to ethical questions;[38] the authoritative pronouncement of the forgiveness of sins;[39] the demand for a personal loyalty to himself breaking through the natural ties of home and kindred;[40] the assertion that God's Kingdom is present and active in his healing works;[41] the parable of the vineyard-owner who sent a succession of messengers to his tenants culminating in the sending of his own son;[42] messianic incidents such as the Transfiguration, the confession of Peter at Caesarea Philippi, the entry into Jerusalem;[43] the increasing, if sometimes veiled, reference to, and emphasis on, his impending death in relation to God's purpose and his own place in it, leading up to the institution of the Last Supper[44]—if, I repeat, these and other things are taken together as elements in a single picture, it is hard, even when full allowance is made for all the difficult critical and exegetical questions in-

---

[37] *Matthew* 4, 19; 16, 24; 19, 21.   [38] *Matthew* 5, 38; 43.

[39] *Mark* 2, 3 ff.   [40] *Luke* 14, 26.   [41] *Matthew* 11, 5; 12, 28.

[42] *Matthew* 21, 33 ff.   [43] *Matthew* 17, 2; 16, 13; 21, 1.

[44] For these references the reader may consult Vincent Taylor, *Jesus and his Sacrifice* (London, Macmillan, 1937), Part II.

volved, to avoid the conclusion stated above, namely, that his own person and men's relation to himself were quite central in his understanding of the way in which men are to be saved. It is hard to believe that all this was read back into the Gospel-picture of Christ by the faith of the infant Church.

(10)

Turning now in a sentence or two to the remainder of the New Testament, we find that what we have said about our Lord's thought of the Kingdom and of his own unique vocation in relation to it has its counterpart there.

Thus first: the New Testament writers, to be sure, make comparatively little use of the concept of the Kingdom as such, and when they do use it, it is mostly in a futurist sense; nevertheless it is plain that they are all deeply conscious of being here and now in this present world in a radically new relation to God. For them the New Age has begun with the advent of Christ, and they have been made participants in it in a new reconciled life of present blessedness, victory and peace. But, on the other hand, they are just as deeply conscious that their salvation is not yet in the fullest sense a present possession. What they have now is an earnest or *arrabon*, a pledge or instalment, of an inheritance to come. And these two things are inseparably bound up with one another in their experience of reconciliation. It is only because they face the challenges and pressures and sufferings of this present life (many of them arising directly from their Christian discipleship) in the light of the divine kingdom which awaits its consummation beyond this present life that they are able to be blessedly and victoriously reconciled to them. But also, it is only because they are being victoriously reconciled to them here and now in this present life that their assurance of the divine kingdom which transcends this present life and in its fulness is yet to be, is so calm and unshakeable and never merely a vague and intermittent dream or an excited, compensatory hope. They live now in the 'powers of the world to come'.[45]

Second—though it seems almost superfluous to say this —all this new life is for the New Testament writers grounded and centred in Christ. Christ is its pattern, source and sustaining power. Christ, and Christ alone, is the Saviour and Reconciler. In short, the New Testament is Christocentric from the first page to the last. Yet, be it noted, it is this without being any the less theocentric. It is *God*, the transcendent and holy, yet loving and merciful, God, who rules over all and 'of whom and through whom and to whom are all things', who has taken action into the world and into human history in Christ the Redeemer and who will at the end 'gather together in one all things in him'. '*God* was in Christ reconciling the world to himself.' The new life is 'hid with Christ in *God*'.[46]

[45] 2 *Corinthians* 1, 22; 5, 5; *Ephesians* 1, 14; *Hebrews* 6, 5; and especially *Romans* 8, 23 ff.

[46] *Ephesians* 1, 10; 2 *Corinthians* 5, 19; *Colossians* 3, 3.

CHAPTER II

CHRIST'S OFFICE AS PROPHET

(1)

WE have said that the vocation of Christ, from the point of view from which we are thinking of it in these lectures, is to be the source and sustainer of the new life, the life reconciled to God, such new life being characterized by the four things summed up on page 26. We have said, too, that into the fulfilment of this vocation his three offices of prophet, priest and king—or rather, to speak more precisely, what we find it convenient compendiously to symbolize by these titles—enter indispensably and inseparably and by it they are held in unity with one another. Together they constitute the 'seamless robe' of his vocation as Reconciler.

This being so, there is, it must be acknowledged, a certain artificiality in separating the three offices from one another. In his reconciling work for a man, Christ does not at one stage fulfil his prophetic office and then at another, demitting this, fulfil his priestly office and then at still another fulfil his kingly office, each to the exclusion of the other two. No doubt, any one of these aspects of Christ's work may sometimes be more prominent than the others, according to a man's special situation and need; nevertheless it is always possible to discern the others entering in in some degree if the need is in fact being deeply and fully met, is being met, that is to say, in the way that it is

Christ's distinctive vocation to meet it. Thus, to refer back to what I said earlier[1] and to anticipate briefly what will emerge more fully later, if we relate the three offices to three fundamental needs of the human spirit (a) the need for truth and enlightenment, corresponding to the prophetic office; (b) the need for forgiveness, corresponding to the priestly office; (c) the need for someone to rule and to empower, corresponding to the kingly office, then it is broadly true to say that if a man is, in the practical business of Christian living, being lifted by Christ out of a merely natural and unregenerate style of life into one which bears the authentic marks of Christ upon it, it is because (a) he is discerning, or rediscerning, truths and realities which apart from Christ he would not discern; (b) he is conscious of being a sinful man under the judgment, and needing and receiving the forgiveness, of God; (c) is deep down persuaded, though he might not express it in these terms, that Christ is Lord and that through faith in, and loyal obedience to, Christ a man becomes one with God's purpose and rule, God's Kingdom, both here and hereafter. These are extremely vague and abstract phrases, but perhaps we may pause for a little to relieve them of some of their vagueness and abstractness by a single concrete illustration.

(2)

Consider that new relation to other persons which we saw[2] is an essential element in the new life of reconciliation, the relation of *agapé*, the love which goes out, costingly if need be, to the other man simply because he is 'there' and not because he is, or is not, this or that sort

[1] See above, p. 6. [2] See above, p. 24 ff.

of person. There can be no question that a serious and committed, and not merely a verbal or sentimental, acknowledgment of this ethic of agapeistic love to all men, the continuous endeavour to give it practical embodiment in attitude and action, *is* a distinctive characteristic of the specifically Christ-style of life. Yet I hazard the generalization that this lies wholly outside the range of the natural, unregenerate man even when he regards himself, or is regarded by others, as a 'good living' person. When it comes to a really crucial test, as for example in relation to one who has wronged, or threatens to wrong, him—an 'enemy'—he does not even see the point of such an ethic; it does not 'add up', as the saying is; it seems to him to be 'nonsense', and even feebly sentimental 'nonsense'. That this is so is evidenced *a fortiori* by the fact that even seriously committed Christians find themselves, in really testing situations, coming close to the natural man in this regard; the ideal and imperative of love seem to them also remote and unreal and utterly beyond their resources, and too often, it is to be feared, they do no more than acquiesce in this. Yet if it be indeed thus beyond even them, if it cannot be fulfilled even to the extent of imparting some degree of Christian novelty to their behaviour, the Sermon on the Mount, the thirteenth chapter of First Corinthians, the twelfth chapter of Romans, and in general the injunction to let 'that mind be in you which was also in Christ Jesus'[3] might as well not be in the New Testament. What then can bring such an agapeistic ethic within the range of the Christian man? It can only come within the scope of practical possibility for him and begin to shape his whole mood and temper, so that men take note of him as being somehow different, as bearing in

[3] *Philippians* 2, 5.

some observable degree the stamp of Christ, if three things are happening in his spirit corresponding with the three needs which we have associated above with the three offices of Christ.

First, he needs to have, and to be able continually to recapture, 'moments of vision' in which he *sees* the other man, and indeed the whole personal order in which he is bound up with that other man and with God, in a new and different light. It is emphatically not a matter of trying to work up, or to simulate, 'gushy' feelings towards him, as we said earlier; it is a matter of discernment, judgment, of seeing the truth, in such a way that the other man becomes to you as it were a different person from the merely odious creature he would otherwise be. It is a matter of 'whereas I was blind, now I see'.[4] And what is seen is, to use the now somewhat cliché, but from the Christian point of view completely realistic, New Testament phrase, 'a brother for whom Christ died'.[5]

Second, he needs to have, and to be able continually to recover, in all his dealings with the other man a humble and penitent sense of being himself a sinful man, of being himself under judgment and needing above all things else, as well as receiving daily, the forgiveness of God. To say this is not to utter a merely conventionally Christian, pietistic sentiment. On the contrary, it expresses something absolutely indispensable in the Christian ethic of love, or rather in the fulfilment of that ethic by the re-conciled man. It would be possible to develop this at some length, but it suffices here to say, linking it up with the last point, that the capacity to *see* the other man as 'a brother for whom Christ died' springs in part from a living, deeply felt, and continually renewed sense of one-

[4] *John* 9, 25.   [5] *Romans* 14, 15; 1 *Corinthians* 8, 11.

self as a sinner for whom Christ died; the two things are inseparably bound up with one another.

Third, he needs to share, to be able continually to re-establish himself in, the faith that agapeistic love, love as revealed and embodied in Christ, is of God, that despite its present apparent foolishness and weakness it wields in the final issue the power of God and will share in the triumph of His Kingdom; the faith, in St John's words (giving full weight to the word *God*) that 'God is love; and he who dwells in love dwells in God, and God in him'.[6] It is very much to be doubted whether it is possible to make and sustain the ventures and take the risks of *agapé* without some such faith, without the deeply felt conviction, however expressed, or perhaps not expressed in terms at all, that *agapé* in spite of the appearances is really a profoundly reasonable way of life, being grounded in reality, the *ultimate* reality, God. I am disposed to think, indeed, that any high ethic which goes beyond group standards and conformities requires for its fulfilment some such 'metaphysical' grounding and context, however dimly grasped; though some would deny this. But however that may be, this, if it is ever true, is certainly true of the ethic of *agapé* as set before us in Christ and in the New Testament. The requirements of such an ethic can run so counter to the immediately observable and calculable factors of human nature and history that it is only by the undergirding of faith in God, in God's rule and victory, that they can evoke, and in spite of all retain, that full measure of devotion and self-commitment which is part of the very definition of Christian living and discipleship. In other words, there must be the faith that Christ is King.

[6] 1 *John* 4, 16.

(3)

There is then a certain artificiality in separating the three offices from one another; nevertheless, for the purposes of reflection and exposition we have to take one thing at a time, and that being so there is good reason for following the traditional order and taking his office as prophet first. For under the symbol of prophet we compendiously sum up that aspect of Christ's saving work which has to do with the effective bringing of the truth, the light of truth, to men in the blindness and darkness and alienation of their minds from God, and that plainly is, and must always be, basic and all-pervasive in what he accomplishes for them. Man—this is a truism, but truisms sometimes need stating—is essentially and by definition a personal being, and a *personal* being is essentially and by definition one who is capable of discerning truth, knowing that he is discerning it, and acting self-consciously and self-directingly in the light of it. A person needs to discern truth as his body needs to consume food; there is for him no movement or growth towards his proper maturity as a personal being to which the words quoted above are not in some degree applicable, 'whereas I was blind, now I see', or the words 'there fell from his eyes as it had been scales'.[7] 'Ye shall know the truth and the truth shall make you free.'[8] We state the same truth from another angle if we say that one reason for taking Christ's office as prophet first is that when we come to speak of his work for us under the symbols of priest and king we must take care to do so always on the broad basis of his prophetic office, his office as light-bringer, as mediator of truth, for only by doing so can we unfailingly bear in mind that at no point does

[7] *Acts* 9, 18.   [8] *John* 8, 32.

Christ's saving work for a man merely override his personal insight and vision; on the contrary it operates always
through the quickening and illumining of them. It never
takes his personal defences by assault, to use one of John
Oman's phrases. Only by insisting on this with ourselves
can we keep our understanding of Christ's work on a
fully personal level and avoid those subtly mechanical
and manipulative interpretations of it which, as the history of thought on these matters shows, so easily creep in.

Because Christ's office as prophet is thus so basic and
all-pervasive it bears upon, and could be illustrated from,
almost any aspect of the reconciled life. We must therefore
select our theme. I propose to do this along a line which is
in harmony with the general course of our thought so far:
I want to do no more than emphasize and illustrate the
importance of always, in our thought about these matters,
keeping Christ's office as prophet in closest relation with
his vocation as the Reconciler—the importance of always
holding together in reciprocal interplay with one another
the *fact*, as we believe it to be, that Christ is uniquely the
mediator of truth to us and the *reason* why he mediates it
—the end in view—namely that he may reconcile us to
God. I will develop this along two lines, the second more
briefly than the first.

(4)

The first is this: by keeping Christ's office as prophet in
closest relation with his vocation as Reconciler we are
enabled to understand why God has given, and gives, the
saving truth to us through a historic human person and
life, the person and life of Jesus of Nazareth; we are
enabled to discern afresh how inseparably bound up with

one another are the Christian Gospel, alike in its content and its power, and the fact that it is rooted and grounded in a historic revelation. Furthermore, and by the same token, we are helped to see the appropriateness of the symbol 'prophet' to describe this aspect of Christ's work. To elucidate these points we must go back again, even at the cost of some repetition, to the four elements in the new and reconciled life which were set forth in the last lecture.

It is not difficult, I think, to see on reflection that all these four aspects of the new life, if they are to be livingly entered into, presuppose and require the apprehension of God as *holy love*.

Thus, first, to be reconciled to God in respect to sin, to be deeply and truly penitent for sin and yet at the same time to be at peace about it before God, is only possible through an apprehension of God as holy love, which because it is *holy* inflexibly exposes and judges the sinner in his lovelessness, disobedience and distrust and yet at the same time because it is *love* holds the sinner to itself in a seeking and pardoning mercy which asks only that the penitent man should commit himself to it in faith. This, of course, is fundamental, and I shall develop it more fully when we come to speak in the next lecture of our Lord's office as priest.

Second, to be reconciled to God in respect of even his austerest requirements upon us, to be *really* reconciled and not merely reluctantly submissive, only becomes possible as a man is able to apprehend that those requirements are not the demands of an inscrutable and impersonal moral order, nor the exactions of a hard and inexorable law-giver with which a man had better comply for fear of punitive consequences, but are rather the divine love itself drawing near to him and calling him into his true blessed-

ness, the blessedness which is to be found only in fellowship with God and in the service of His purpose in the
world in obedience and trust.

Third, to be reconciled to all God's appointments, even
the most grievously painful and frustrating, to be *really*
reconciled to them, to be 'more than conqueror over
them', and not merely to capitulate to them in a dull
acquiescence or a stony stoicism or a smouldering resentment only becomes possible as a man is able to accept
them as from the hand of a divine love and an overshadowing presence and providence which are wholly to be
trusted even when the way of their working is utterly
baffling and mysterious.

Fourth, to be reconciled to God in and through the new
relation of *agapé* to other persons is only possible, as was
said earlier in this lecture, if a man is brought to see them
in a new light, the light of God's own holy will of love rest-
ing upon them and meeting and claiming him through them.

This brings us to the crucial question. How could such
a living apprehension of, and faith in, God as holy love
ever come to possess a man's spirit, not merely occasionally
and intermittently at moments of rare exaltation of feeling
but continually in relation to all the contingencies, challenges and pressures, even the worst, that life has to offer?
The answer is that God Himself should make *effective* revelation of Himself as holy love—effective, that is to say,
in relation to man's actual situation in this so shadowed
and distressful world. If this be granted, how else, we must
then ask, could such a revelation be thus effectively made
than through a fully human and historic person who does
not merely announce and talk about the love of God,
however eloquently, but is himself utterly possessed and
controlled by and surrendered to it; how else, that is to

say, than through a perfectly reconciled, historic human life encountering men in the midst of and out of the midst of concrete actualities which constitute their historical existence as human persons and in relation to which their reconciliation, in all its four basic aspects, must be continuously realized. In particular we must emphasize again what I have written elsewhere, that the revelation must come to us in the midst of and out of the midst of human, personal life as darkened and perverted and embittered by men's sin and folly, for it is in the midst of it as so darkened and perverted and embittered by sin that the reconciled man, himself a sinner, is called to live the new life with God.[9]

(5)

We have urged that God's revelation of Himself as holy love, to be effectively reconciling, must have taken the historic, personal form which it actually did take in Christ. How else, we have asked, could it have taken place? as though the answer to the question were self-evident. But, it may be asked, is it self-evident? Must we not be wary of making such retrospective inference, of turning what has happened, or is believed to have happened, into a discernible prior necessity that it should so happen? Who are we, it might be said, to say what God must do for 'us men and our salvation'? It is at least abstractly and theoretically conceivable that God, with Whom all things are possible, might have devised some other method of making an effective revelation of His nature as love and so made possible our reconciliation.

[9] See my *God and Men* (London, James Nisbet & Co. Ltd, pp. 95 ff.) for a fuller exposition of the view outlined above.

He might have caused the truth to be oracularly pro-
claimed through some mouthpiece whose authority was
compellingly established by signs, portents and miracles
and accompanied by some direct, internal manipulation
of men's minds. Such notions of divine revelation have
indeed been not uncommon throughout the history of
religion and have even entered into the interpretation of
Christ's saving work. Two things may be said about this.
First, if our appeal is in a sense to 'self-evidence', that is
not intended to mean more than that there is a certain
discernible fitness between the manner of the revelation
of the divine love and that reconciliation which it makes
possible and actual in men's lives and which, therefore, we
must believe, it was intended by God to make possible and
actual. The argument does no more—yet how much that
is—than point to the massive and impressive unity and
consistency of Christian truth, a unity and consistency
which, it may be suggested, constitutes in part its uniqueness and convincing power. Second (though this is perhaps only to develop the same point a little farther), the
notion that the truth that God is holy love might be in
some way authoritatively announced and men's minds
overridingly compelled into believing it masks a material,
though not logically formal, self-contradiction. For to love
a person—*really* to love him in the full and perfect meaning of the term 'love' which it must bear when it is applied
to God—whatever else it must connote and include, must
signify an undeviating respect for him *as a person*, as a
being, that is to say, who is in some real and ultimate sense
in charge of his own destiny and under call to walk in
freedom by his own insight and discernment of reality
and truth. The desire merely to manipulate and override,
or otherwise manage, a person even for his own good is a

contradiction and denial of love itself, though in men's unregenerate relations with one another it often masquerades as love. Much that men rate as love is often, in fact and in greater or less degree, an unconscious instrument and exercise of power. The notion, then, that God might have in some way imposed on, or implanted in, the minds of sinful men for their good the truth that he is love is self-contradictory. A saving revelation of love which worked thus would not in fact be revelation of love, nor would it be saving.

(6)

It is perhaps not superfluous to point out how consonant all this is with the spirit and outlook of Christ as he meets us in the Gospels. Though he was aware of his unique vocation in the counsels of God and the destinies of men, though he knew that the 'Kingdom of God' had broken savingly into the world in a unique and once-for-all way in himself, there is nevertheless a complete, deliberate and explicit rejection of any attempt to impose himself, his teaching and claims, upon men, to coerce them into surrender, whether by promise or threat, or authoritarian command, or overwhelming portent, or some other exercise of spectacular power. His so-called 'miracles' were plainly the inevitable, one might say unstudied, outflow of his love for men and an expression of the living presence and power of God now being manifested in his own person and vocation—in a sense he could not help doing them; yet at the same time he was plainly anxious lest they should cause men to attach themselves to him without any real insight into his primary message and call.[10] Any attempt thus to establish an ascendancy in

[10] One may cite his injunction to those whom he healed 'to tell no man'

the lives of men he appears once and for all to have rejected in what we call the Temptation, the account of
which, when read in the light of his consciousness of his
unique vocation, has such a realistic subtlety that its
essence, if not its precise form, must surely be taken to have
come in the first instance from his own lips.[11] The same
point emerges when we note that Christ nowhere lays
down regulations or issues directives for conduct except
in terms that plainly are not intended to do more than
present a certain distinctive style of life and a call for
personal insight and decision in the pursuit of it; nor,
needless to say, is there any attempt to formulate a systematic, authoritative body of teaching. His characteristic method of teaching is by parable and his reiterated
appeal is to those who have ears to hear, to hear. 'The
great demonstration of the Christ', writes John Oman, 'is
just that he never sets himself, as the absolute external
authority of the perfect truth, in opposition to the imperfect authority of the finite and sinful spirit within, but
that he has only one appeal, which is to the likeness of
God and the teaching of God within. Jesus speaks indeed
with authority. He is not as the scribes. They had authori-
ties, but no authority. They had nothing to speak from
direct, and nothing to speak to direct. Jesus, on the other
hand, speaks from man to man the truth he has seen
and to which his hearers cannot be blind unless they
close their eyes. . . . His "I say unto you" did not end

(*Matthew* 8, 4; 9, 30), his repudiation of those who sought from him a sign
from heaven (*Matthew* 12, 38 ff.; *Mark* 8, 12); his apparent shrinking from the
multitudes that sometimes followed him, and his addressing to them of some
of his most demanding sayings as though deliberately to check such crowd-
excitement (*Matthew* 8, 18; *Luke* 14, 25 ff.).

[11] *Matthew* 4, 1 ff.; *Luke* 4, 1 ff.

enquiry, but begin it. Hear something, it said, which the humble heart will recognize as true, and which the experience of obedience will confirm. And surely herein is the weightiest proof of the perfect truth. It does not dominate and silence the inward voices, but awakes them and makes them its chief witness.'[12]

(7)

We can now see how appropriate the term 'prophet' is as the compendious and epitomizing symbol for all this aspect of Christ's reconciling work. By 'prophet' we mean one who comes bearing and expressing the truth of God not in words only, however eloquent, but also and much more in and through his own person in the way we have described. He speaks from an inward vision and under an inward compulsion which do not in any sense or any degree negate or by-pass his personal being but rather is one with it, quickening and intensifying it. He is himself wholly possessed and fashioned by the truth which he brings, and that, too, not in isolation from the historical context but in living relation with it, in living relation with the actual situations which confront and challenge both him and those to whom he speaks; in an indefinable but real way he is identified with the truth, possesses and is possessed by it in himself, 'incarnates' it, and his message draws its uniquely self-authenticating, illuminating and recreative power from that fact. This is undoubtedly the New Testament way of thinking of Christ as the source of saving truth, even though the fully developed New Testament faith concerning him, as it meets us in the

[12] J. Oman, *Vision and Authority* (London, Hodder & Stoughton, 2nd ed., 1928), pp. 107, 112.

Epistles, nowhere in fact applies the concept 'prophet' to his person and work.[13]

This points to the answer we must give to those in whom the application of the term 'prophet' to Christ may perhaps cause some uneasiness because they feel that it assimilates him too much to Old Testament prophecy and so fails to do justice to the full Christian faith concerning his unique person and work. The answer is, first, that we are here using the symbol 'prophet' to indicate only one aspect of his saving and reconciling vocation and work. We have yet to take up his offices as priest and as king. Second, that while it is true that in using the term prophet we do in one way assimilate Christ to the Old Testament prophets and are content so to do for the reason just indicated, namely that it is the mark of the prophet that his message and his person are fused together and become one, yet in another sense we do not do so, for Christ and his message are one with a fulness and completeness which transcend the Old Testament prophets. While the latter were constituted prophets by the fact that they were deeply and inwardly possessed by the truth they uttered, such 'possession' was 'occasional', not in any pejorative sense of that term, but simply in the sense that when it occurred it did so, so to say, only *ad hoc*, i.e. in relation to the particular historical occasions and situations to which they spoke. Christ's possession by and revelation of the truth, on the other hand, we have every reason to think was a continuous and uninterrupted

[13] In the New Testament the term occurs, in relation to Christ's ministry, only in the Gospels, and there, with but one or two exceptions, it is used by those who, deeply impressed by his teaching and works, had, apparently, no more adequate category to apply to him (*Matthew* 14, 5; 21, 11 & 46). The disciples, too, seem to have thought of him, in the first instance, as a prophet (*Luke* 24, 19).

manifestation of his whole personal being. It shone through every aspect and activity, even the relatively transient and trivial, of his being and life, through everything that he was and stood for and said and did and suffered. The whole of him was involved, at all times and in all contingencies. This contrast with the Old Testament prophets receives perhaps its most impressive exemplification in his Passion. We may set alongside one another Jeremiah's cry, 'Cursed be the day in which I was born! The day my mother bore me, let it not be blessed! Why did I come forth from the womb to see toil and sorrow, and spend my days in shame?'[14] and the cry of dereliction from the Cross, 'My God, my God, why hast thou forsaken me?'[15] The former cry is sheerly and rebelliously tragic and calamitous as the latter cry, however it is interpreted, manifestly is not for it is addressed to '*my* God, *my* God'. To recall what was said earlier[16]—the 'my', we dare think, points to a deeper, underlying and essentially unimpaired faith in and commitment to God which in the bitter anguish of the hour was wrestling through to its unclouded expression in the final words, 'Father, into thy hands I commend my spirit'.[17]

[14] *Jeremiah* 20, 14–18 (R.S.V.).

[15] *Mark* 15, 34.   [16] See above, p. 24.

[17] *Luke* 23, 46. The force of the contrast we have drawn is not essentially weakened by the fact that the cry of dereliction is a quotation from *Psalms* 22,1 and that in that Psalm we are confronted with a godly man who in the midst of dire persecution and suffering does not in fact echo Jeremiah's cry but wins through to faith and commitment to God. And indeed it may well have been, as many scholars have suggested, that our Lord in his bitter anguish was consciously finding help in the words of the Psalm, and in so doing took upon his own lips its poignant opening phrases. Yet we must maintain that the contrast still remains; indeed, so far from being essentially weakened it is strengthened by being taken to a deeper level. This becomes evident if we seek imaginatively to grasp so far as we can *all* that the Cross in its starkly horrible actuality must have been to his acute sensitivity, and *all* that is meant by the words 'my spirit' when he said, 'Father, into thy

'I am the truth.'[18] Some may question whether these
words ascribed to Jesus in the fourth Gospel can confi-
dently be regarded as having fallen from his lips in that
precise form. But however that may be, there can be, in
the light of what we have been saying, no question of their
appropriateness and truth. They have a deeper authen-
ticity than that of verbally accurate reportage. And one
thing they plainly do: without in the least detaching
Christ from the grand, historical succession of the prophets, they nevertheless decisively and finally separate
him from them. For none of them ever said, or could
have said with the least show of justification, '*I am* the
truth.' Being thus in himself the fulness of truth, he brings
that noble historical succession to its end in both senses of
the word 'end'; he both completes and fulfils it and brings
it to its close.[19]

---

hands I commend my spirit.' We must emphasize the statement already
made that the *whole* of him was always involved in everything that he was
and said and did and suffered. In commending his spirit into his Father's
hands he was commending into those hands all that his spirit, throughout his
ministry, had in his full and perfect love continuously taken upon itself of the
sorrow and sin and disease and heartbreak, the deep and desperate need, of
men and women and had sought in all that he said and did to overcome. *All*
this—now focused and concentrated and summed up in the anguish of Calvary—was on his spirit, was part of his very being, and this spirit he now at
the end commits to God. There is not strictly any parallel to this in the Old
Testament, though there are pointers towards it in this 22nd Psalm and even
more in the 53rd chapter of Isaiah.

[18] *John* 14, 6.

[19] In connection with the application of the term 'prophet' both to the
Old Testament prophets and to Christ, we may add that Christ himself
on one or two occasions seems to have classed himself with the prophets
(*Luke* 4, 24; 13, 33; *Matthew* 13, 57). On the other hand, his awareness of his
unique vocation (see above, p. 31 f.) clearly implies an awareness of his difference from them. This comes to almost explicit expression in his words
about John the Baptist (*Matthew* 11, 1 ff.). If John was a prophet and more
than a prophet, *a fortiori* he to whom it was John's vocation to point was a
prophet and more than a prophet.

(8)

This leads us into the second line of thought which we said we would briefly pursue in connection with the importance of keeping Christ's office as prophet in close relation with his vocation as Reconciler.

The complete adequacy and finality which the Christian faith thus ascribes to the divine revelation in Christ and which is implicit in the words 'I am the truth' has been, and is, sometimes demurred to for one or both of two reasons. The first reason was in substance urged as long ago as the second century by the pagan philosopher Celsus. It is that there is an intrinsic absurdity and incredibility in the assertion that a full, final and once-for-all revelation of God to men should have been made through a Jew of the first century, living in an obscure corner of the world amidst the narrow limitations and restrictions of Jewish life, sharing the beliefs and thought-forms of that age, beliefs and thought-forms which later generations in so many ways have passed beyond. It is unfortunate that the weight and validity of this demurrer have at times been conceded by Christians themselves in that they have sometimes sought to counter it by in effect maintaining that Christ, being divine, was not in fact thus restricted to the mental horizons of his own time, and that everything he believed and said must be held to be free from ignorance and error and therefore accepted without question. But both the objection and this way of meeting it are seen to be misconceived when they are set in the light of what he actually came to reveal and the reconciling work which he came to accomplish. As we have said, it is an essential and central part of his vocation as Reconciler to unveil to men the truth that God is holy love in such a way that they are brought into a new and reconciled life with God *here and now*, that is to say, under historical conditions amidst the restrictions and relativities, the changes and chances and transiencies, of their terrestrial existence in time and space. To have come in any other way than as subject to these conditions would have concealed the very thing which was to be unveiled and so made impossible the very reconciliation it was intended to accomplish.

Indeed, we in these days might well give thanks that Christ lived and taught in the midst of a relatively simple age and society such as those of Palestine in the first century. No doubt we must not exaggerate the simplicity of that age and society. It does not require much knowledge of the contemporary history of that time, or much reading between the lines of the Gospel narratives, to discern that life for a Jew in Palestine at that time was under the constant pressure of social, political and national, as well as of personal, problems. Still, it was in comparison with ours a relatively simple age. One sometimes hears it urged that it is precisely this relative simplicity which makes it difficult for the modern man to find in the Gospels anything that appears to him to be importantly relevant to the major problems of his own life. As he turns his mind from the vast chaos and complex confusion of these times, daily spread before him in the newspaper and the news-bulletins, to the Gospel stories, particularly those highly sentimentalized and falsified versions of them which he probably still carries with him from Sunday-school days, he may well feel that he has passed into another and irrelevant world, one that does not, so to say, 'bite into' his real situation as twentieth-century man. It would not be difficult to show, I think, that this feeling is rooted in a profound misapprehension of the content and meaning of the Gospel story. But leaving that on one side, the point I want to make is that if we are to have a right apprehension of that content and meaning, in terms, that is to say, of the reconciled life exhibited to us there in Christ, the argument might well run in the reverse direction. Granting the *relative* simplicity of the Gospel setting we might well argue that such simplicity is precisely what we in our highly complex age and life need, if the revelation in Christ is to lay hold of us reconcilingly at all. A revelation calculated to pierce our darkness, a darkness in part engendered by the utter confusion of our time, as the confusion is itself in part reciprocally engendered by the darkness in which we dwell, needs to be made in a simpler historical diction and idiom. The canvas, to change the metaphor, had better not be too crowded.

(9)

The second reason for the demurrer is of the same order and is to be met in the same way, that is, by insisting again on the necessity of keeping Christ's office as prophet in inseparable connection with his vocation and work as Reconciler. I have written of this elsewhere, but perhaps I may be permitted to repeat what I have said for the sake of completeness in the present discussion.

It is urged that the Christian claim that in Christ there is given to us a full and final revelation of truth is unreasonable to the point of absurdity for the reason that man's experience and knowledge in all spheres have continuously moved forward all down the centuries and are still doing so. If any one were to claim in respect of any branch of knowledge that his teaching, or that of anybody else, was final, we would dismiss the claim as absurd

and hardly worth serious consideration. How prepos-
terous, then, to ask us to believe that the truth which comes
to us in Christ, great and valuable as it may be, introduces
a finality into our knowledge of the infinite reality of God.
At first hearing this seems to have force. But in fact when
the Christian claim concerning the truth given in Christ
is rightly understood, understood, that is to say, in the
light of his vocation as the Reconciler, the objection has no
weight. It really misses the main point. For it fails to take
account of the profound difference between the sources of
knowledge in the personal world, the world of persons in
relation with one another and with God, and the sources of
knowledge in other spheres. The Christian claim for Christ
is not that he provides information about God of a kind
that can be comprehended and stated in propositions to
which further propositions can be added in the same way
as the scientist provides information about the behaviour
of, say, atoms. No, the claim is that Christ *reconciles men to
God* and that basically there his finality lies. Of course, the
claim may be questioned or rejected, but it must be questioned and rejected in terms of the actual claim that is
made. Viewed thus, the finality of Christ cannot be thought
of as putting a premature limit to our knowledge of God;
rather it must be thought of as doing the exact opposite; it
takes the limits off. It is the state of unreconciliation, and
the consequent 'alienation from the life of God'[20] which
closes the avenues to such knowledge, and it is the state
of reconciliation which opens them up. Christ's finality
is his finality as healer of blindness and darkness and
ignorance, as *source* of light and truth in this sphere.[21]

[20] *Ephesians* 4, 18.
[21] See my *God and Men* (London, James Nisbet & Co. Ltd, 1948), p. 94.

E

CHAPTER III

CHRIST'S OFFICE AS PRIEST

(1)

UNDER the symbol of priest it is our purpose to explore further the first of the four aspects of reconciliation to God of which we have spoken—reconciliation to Him, being at peace with Him, in respect of sin. The symbol of priest directs our thought once again to the central paradox of Christ's saving relation to men, namely, that he continually evokes in them a deep sense of sinfulness and yet also at the same time an equally deep sense of being at peace with God about it. This double aspect of Christ's work finds appropriate expression in the symbol in question. In the history of religion it has always been a distinctive function of the priest to act in some sort as an intermediary between men and God. As such he both sets men and God apart and unites them together; his office expresses and emphasizes the truth that there is a gulf between them and that it is both bridgeable and bridged.

It has been the endeavour of what Bagehot called 'experiencing natures' to do justice to this double, paradoxical impact of Christ upon them which has lain behind the age-long wrestling with theories of the atonement and also the form the theories have taken. It is not my purpose to expound and explore these theories, but perhaps I can best make clear what my purpose is by beginning with the familiar fact that historically such theories have tended to fall into two broad classes. Obviously the relation of estrangement between God and man brought about by man's sin involves the two factors named, God and man. The question then is how do each of these two stand in a change from the relation of estrangement to one of restored fellowship, of reconciliation, what conditions need to be fulfilled in respect of each. Obviously there must be a change in the sinner. There must be brought about in him a profound change of mind, a *metanoia*, to use the New Testament term, a facing in a new direction; in short, a deep and genuine repentance. There has never been any difference of view about that; all doctrines of atonement have it in common. The debated point has been whether anything more is required, whether it is necessary for Christ, in order to reconcile the sinner to God, to effect something else in addition to bringing about a change in him, something which is in some way directed to the other factor in the relation, God himself.

Here the views divide, and the two broad classes to which I have referred appear. On the one hand, there is the view which says that nothing more is required than to bring about the indispensable change in the mind of sinful man and that Christ's work is to bring about the change in so profound a way that he is *eo facto* put on an entirely new footing with God of forgiveness and reconciliation. On the other hand, there is the view which maintains that such a change in man, whilst of course indispensable, is not sufficient; something else in addition is required. This something else is necessary because one term in the relation is *God*; it is something directed towards God's holy will, and not merely to man's unholy will. Indeed, on this view, it is in part because Christ fulfils this other requirement towards God that he is able

to fulfil the first requirement and bring about the necessary change in men. It is in part because the sinner becomes aware of Christ doing this thing towards God on
his behalf, fulfilling this indispensable condition of his
forgiveness which he himself could never fulfil, that his
whole attitude is transformed. As to what this further
thing is which Christ in his reconciling work effects, this
has been variously conceived in the different theories.

It has always seemed to me a somewhat odd and challenging thing that these two different ways of thinking
about Christ's reconciling work in the forgiveness of sins
should have emerged and persisted all down the history of
Christian thought on these matters. For it does not appear
that the difference corresponds to, or is reflected in, a
difference in the degree in which the reconciling work of
Christ in forgiveness is actually entered into and ap-
propriated and enjoyed. Some of the greatest Christian
saints I have ever known, men and women whose whole
being and life have been centred in and fashioned by their
experience of the forgiveness of sins through Christ, have
never, on their own confession, been in the least conscious that there was any need for Christ to do more for
them than what he actually has done and does do for
them, namely, to bring them as sinners to, and to keep
them in, a state of deep and true penitence in the presence
of God, a state in which they are assured and continually
reassured of God's forgiveness, and so find themselves reconciled and at peace. On the other hand, I have known
many of like quality of Christian experience and life who
have clearly felt very deeply that without this thought of
Christ doing something on their behalf, something directed
Godwards which they themselves could never do, they
would not know the peace of sins forgiven at all. The for-

mer find it difficult to understand what the latter are so concerned about; the latter find it difficult to understand why the former are not concerned about it. It is certainly rather odd, to say the least. One has only to set alongside of one another in imagination really great Christian personalities and thinkers like, say, John Oman and James Denney to feel the full force of this. Now what I am leading up to in all this is this: it seems to me that we must try so to enter into Christ's reconciling work for us in respect of sin that we can see that both these ways of understanding and formulating it are true at one and the same time, both the way that says that nothing more is necessary for Christ to do for us than to bring us to a true and deep penitence, and the way that says that it is also necessary for Christ to do something on our behalf towards God. That sounds contradictory, but it is not really so. I want to suggest that concerning Christ's reconciling work in respect of sin, it is perfectly true to say that no more is necessary than to bring us to and keep us in a true and deep penitence. But then I want also to suggest, that if we then go on to ask *how* Christ thus brings the sinner to such penitence, it becomes necessary to say in answer to the question that he does so through something which he is doing all the time *towards* God in and through the very act of bringing the sinner to repentance. Thus in one sense all he does is to bring the sinner to and keep him in a state of true and deep penitence; yet in another sense that is not all that he does, for if he is to do exactly that, then in the doing of it he must do something else towards God. I must now try to elucidate these perhaps somewhat cryptic and complex remarks.

(2)

We may note, first, that these two apparently opposed strands of thought are to be discerned in the life and teaching of our Lord as set before us in the Gospels. *On the one hand*, there does not appear to be in the Gospels any hint that anything more is necessary for the forgiveness of a man's sins, for bringing him into a new, reconciled relation to God, than that he should be deeply penitent and humbly cast himself upon the mercy of God. That the divine forgiveness waits only upon penitence and goes forth instantly and self-revealingly to meet it not only finds expression in Christ's explicit teaching as in the parables of the Prodigal Son and of the Pharisee and the Publican[1] but also shines forth in his personal attitude to and dealing with men and women—the paralytic young man let down through the roof; the woman who washed his feet with her tears; Peter, when he cried 'depart from me for I am a sinful man, Lord'; Zacchaeus, the penitent thief.[2] This must surely be significant. It is hard to think that if there really is in the personal order in which God

[1] *Luke* 15, 11 ff.; 18, 10 ff. Cf. also *Luke* 15, 7: 'Joy shall be in heaven over one sinner that repenteth.'

[2] *Matthew* 9, 2; *Luke* 7, 36; 5, 9; 19, 5; 23, 43. In the first of these incidents there is no indication that the young man was conscious of himself not only as a sick man needing healing but also as a sinful man needing forgiveness; but it is a safe inference that he was poignantly aware of both needs—this in view of current teaching at the time that disease was due to a man's sin, and in view of Christ's sensitive, imaginative and intuitive insight into the thoughts and feelings of those with whom he was dealing and the almost tender tone of his words, as reported in St Matthew's Gospel, which might be translated 'Cheer up, sonny, thy sins are forgiven thee'. (Cf. J. A. Findlay, *Jesus as they saw Him*, pp. 46, 290, Epworth Press, 1920.) But even if we assume, in default of evidence to the contrary, that the man's mind was possessed only by the desire to be healed, the argument holds; for the pronouncement of forgiveness going forth to such an one would *a fortiori* go forth to one who gave evidence of being genuinely penitent for his sin.

has set men something essential, fundamental, so to say structural, which ineluctably requires something else to be done before even the most deeply and sincerely penitent man can be received and forgiven of God, something as *tremendous*, in the full and literal sense of that very overworked word, as the Cross, this should not have been discerned by one who is otherwise so unerringly perceptive of the realities of God and man and of their relation to one another, and found expression in his teaching. *On the other hand*, it is equally difficult in the light of the Gospel records, even when every allowance has been made for the critical questions involved, to avoid the conclusion that our Lord thought of his Passion, culminating in the Cross, as in some sense a representative and vicarious offering of himself to God on behalf of sinful men.[3] This thought of Christ offering himself to God as a 'sacrifice' for sin occurs also—though rarely—elsewhere in the New Testament.[4] But neither in the Gospels nor in the Epistles is there any clear indication how this 'sacrificial' self-offering is to be interpreted. We are left then with the paradox already stated on our hands, namely, that penitence is all that is necessary for forgiveness and that at the same time our Lord in fulfilling his vocation was deeply conscious of a compulsion laid upon him to offer himself representatively to God on sinful men's behalf. We must, therefore, ourselves seek to bring the two things as best we may into relation with one another.

(3)

First, let us explore for a little the requirement that if a

[3] See Vincent Taylor, *Jesus and his Sacrifice* (London, Macmillan, 1937), pp. 269 ff.

[4] 1 *Corinthians* 5, 7; *Ephesians* 5, 2; *Hebrews* 10, 5–18.

man is to be forgiven, reconciled to God, in respect of his sinfulness, he must be sincerely and truly penitent towards God. What we have to realize is that this is a stupendously difficult requirement to fulfil. Indeed, as we shall see, it is a requirement which in one sense he cannot fulfil and cannot hope to fulfil; yet fulfil it in some sense he must. The immense difficulty of fulfilling this requirement becomes apparent if we focus our minds on the three terms *sincere*, *true* and *towards God*. Penitence of a sort, penitence to which none of these adjectives properly applies, is relatively easy to achieve. The view that the divine forgiveness waits only upon penitence is sometimes criticized on the ground that it makes such forgiveness cheap and easy. The criticism cannot be admitted. On the contrary, it may be thought to rest on a rather cheap and easy and shallow view of sin and of its consequences in the human spirit. When you begin really to understand what sin is and what it does in and to the human person you begin to see that to bring a man to, and continually to renew in him, a really sincere and true penitence towards God is an infinitely difficult and costing task. It requires in fact, as I shall maintain, nothing less and nothing other than the total self-offering of the Saviour himself to God.

Consider first, then, what we mean by *sincere* penitence towards God. By *sincere* penitence towards God we mean a penitence which springs continuously from a genuinely personal vision of what we are and where we stand in relation to God's holy will of love, and not from any merely artificial or auto-suggestive or transient excitement of feeling. The temptation is great, especially if we are of a certain temperament, when once it is grasped that what is required of us is penitence, to seek to work up, or have worked up in us, what we take to be appropriate feelings of guilt, shame, remorse, contrition, self-reproach, and to suppose that the more demonstratively we can contrive to do this, the more entitled we are, and the more likely, to receive God's pardon. We bid ourselves, or are bidden, to confess ourselves 'miserable offenders', 'all our righteousness as filthy rags', and we proceed liturgically to do so in elegantly phrased catalogues of our sins and shortcomings in what are sometimes commended as 'beautiful' prayers; but the unreality that lurks in it all is shown by the fact that on the one hand we feel a certain glow of self-satisfaction pervading our protestations of self-dissatisfaction, a sense almost of now deserving God's forgiveness by virtue of our emphatic repudiation of all deserving, and that on the other hand we should be indignant if directly we came from worship someone in the church porch began to say about us even a tenth of the things we have just so blandly said about ourselves in what we have declared to be the presence of God. Few things indeed more reveal the often bogus superficiality of our awareness of ourselves as sinful men and women than our intense and instant resentment of any criticism of our behaviour by other people. Or, if we are of a more extroverted temperament, we may perhaps react against the whole business and say in effect: 'I do not feel like that at all; I am not conscious of being a miserable sinner and I am going to cease pretending that I do.' That has the sound of honesty, and in comparison with what has gone before, it may be at least a little more honest; but the man who takes that line may still be in as unreal a world as the man who works himself up, or is worked up, to an artificial ecstasy of guilt-feeling and self-condemnation. An extravagance of penitence, or of what is thought to be penitence, and a coldness which feels no penitence and no inclination even to simulate it, may equally evidence the falsity and unreality of the world in which a man is living. This has brought us, second, to the meaning of what I have called a true penitence towards God.

(4)

By *true* penitence I mean a penitence which springs from a judgment upon ourselves which is in accord with the actualities of the personal order and of the divine will and purpose in relation to that order and is *not* based on some other standards of our own. A man may not be artificially working up in himself feelings of moral and spiritual failure and inferiority—such feelings may come quite spontaneously and unbidden—yet the standards by which he is unconsciously judging and from which his feelings spring may be false wholly or in part. Thus a man's feeling of dissatisfaction with himself is often in greater or lesser degree merely the reflection of other people's estimate of him or what he takes to be such. When others approve of him he is less disturbed about himself; or on the other hand, when he is depressed by some failure to be all that he would like to be in the presence and the presumed estimate of his fellows, he is ready, under appropriate stimulus, for any amount of self-depreciation concerning his sinful condition. On either count he is far from the difficult sanity and objectivity of Thomas à Kempis when he wrote 'thou art not the more holy for being praised; nor the more worthless for being dispraised; what thou art that thou art in the sight of God'. And again, 'whether men judge well of thee, or ill, thou art not on that account other than thyself'.[5] Again, a great many people's concern

[5] *Of the Imitation of Christ*, Bk. 2, Ch. 6; Bk. 3, Ch. 28.

about their sinful shortcomings springs in large measure from a disguised and subtle egotism and pride. They have perhaps, particularly if they have had a Christian up-bringing and take their Christian profession seriously, formed an image of themselves as displaying an exalted Christian character, and when they find, as they inevitably do, that they persistently fall short of this 'ego-ideal', they are cast down and depressed and harassed with guilt-feelings. This they mistake for a true and deep penitence, but it may be little more than a feeling of injured pride, of disappointed *amour propre* and self-esteem. It is possible for a man to be concerned even about his egotism in a thoroughly egotistic way, so complex and deceitful is the human heart.

(5)

Third, *towards God*—the meaning of this phrase in rela-tion to sincere and true penitence for sin has obviously underlain and been contained in what has already been said. Sin, it is hardly necessary to say, is essentially a religious category and is not properly to be used except in respect of a man's relation to *God*; hence it has not been possible for us to describe and define sincere and true penitence except by reference, implicit or explicit, to that relation. If now we add this further word, it is in order to make clear and to emphasize that the sincere and true penitence to which the divine word of forgiveness comes is not fully comprehended in the sort of abstract, verbal description and explication we have given even though there is implicit in these an underlying reference to God. What we have to realize is that there enters into sincere and true penitence in greater or lesser degree—the more it is sincere and true, the greater the degree—a dread sense of having set oneself in one's sinning against the Lord and Source of all being and in particular against the Lord and Source of one's own being—against the ultimate Power who holds one in the hollow of his hand, with whom one's whole existence and destiny are fatefully and ineluctably bound up, to whom is due that total surrender and obedience which in one's sinning has been withheld. We are here in the realm of the profoundest feeling apprehension of God *as God*, and therefore what we have in mind is beyond adequate expression in terms; hence we can perhaps best indicate it by a concrete instance. Consider the poignant expression of penitence in the 51st Psalm, particularly in the words of verse 4, 'against thee, thee *only*, have I sinned and done that which is evil in thy sight'. We must focus our minds on the word 'only'. If, for our purpose here, we accept the tradition that the Psalm was wrung from David by remorse for the wicked thing he did to Uriah and Bathsheba, the word 'only' seems singularly inappropriate and misleading. He had sinned against Uriah and Bathsheba, sinned abominably. Why, then, against God *only*? Because, we must reply, to the religiously awakened and penitent mind the peculiar significance of his sin, that which essentially constitutes it *sin*, does not reside in the relation in which it involves him with his fellows, deplorable as these may be, but in the relation in which it inevitably involves him with God. Sin, of course, has to do with human relations; it has no practical content apart from them; but for the religious mind it runs out far beyond them into the very being and heart of God, and only because it thus runs out far beyond them is it specifically and awfully 'sin' in his experience and destiny. On the lips of the deeply penitent religious man therefore the cry 'against thee, thee *only*, have I sinned' might almost seem to be an exactly and literally true statement.

Some such awareness as this, however expressed, or perhaps not expressed or even expressible in terms at all but only felt, some sense that because of one's sin the very foundation of one's being and life has been shaken (for what is God if not the very foundation of one's being and life?), some consciousness that sin holds one suspended not over the shallows of time but over the abyss of eternity, the abyss of God, is an element in sincere and true penitence towards God; it is in fact this consciousness which in part constitutes it *towards God*. Where such a sense appears to be lacking, the only appropriate comment would seem to be Anselm's: '*nondum consideras ti quanti ponderis sit peccatum*'.[6]

(6)

One thing emerges from all this: no man can command at will this profound re-orientation of mind and spirit, this *metanoia*, this sincere and true penitence towards God. He cannot with any hope of success simply say to himself in effect, I am 'fed-up' with myself and my present manner of life; I will now make a completely fresh start and facing frankly the realities of my inner being and outward behaviour detach myself from them and set off brightly in a new direction. After the first World War the Church of England announced a great mission of repentance in which all its members were called to take part. 'Curious idea,' commented the late Principal

---

[6] *Cur Deus Homo*, I, 21: 'You have not yet considered the exceeding gravity of sin.'

Skinner to me in that slightly caustic manner which so often gave edge to a keen and searching spiritual judgment, 'curious idea to decide in March to repent in October!' And how futile it can be merely to exhort ourselves or other people, in the manner of a certain type of gospel meeting, to repent, repent, repent. The outcome so often is just those artificial feelings of which I have spoken, changing perhaps sooner or later to a chill indifference when the mind cannot find any more reservoirs of feeling within itself from which to pump up penitence on demand. It seems clear that the only way in which we can be continuously brought to such deep and true penitence towards God is for God Himself so to take action, Himself livingly and compellingly so to encounter us, that on the one hand our falsities and self-deceptions are repeatedly broken through and we see ourselves as we really are in his sight, and, on the other hand, the motives for falsity and self-deception, for being other than humbly accepting of what is thus laid bare to us, are removed.

(7)

This brings us back to Christ's reconciling work. It is an essential part of that work that he does for a man the two things just referred to: he discloses to him, and utterly condemns, his sinfulness, and yet at the same time enables him humbly and truthfully to endorse and accept the disclosure and the condemnation. This he does by virtue of the fact that in him there encounters the sinner the holy love of God; not a proposition about the love of God but the holy love itself in a living and wholly unclouded personal embodiment in the midst of the actual relations and conditions of man's sinful, historical existence. Such holy love, being holy, most searchingly reveals and judges what a man in fact is in his unholiness; but also, being love, it grapples him to itself even in the act of so revealing and judging, and in so doing strikes at the root of that blind and blinding self-deception and insincerity which are part of the very essence and power of sin. At the root of all self-deception and insincerity there lies a deep-seated, egocentric anxiety and fear. But if God is indeed holy love, and livingly apprehended as such in Christ, then there is now nothing to fear, not even the devastating condemnation which that love carries with it, nothing we need to deceive ourselves about. We can open all cupboards and fear no skeletons. 'There is no fear in love, but perfect love casts out fear.'[7]

Thus to apprehend the utter condemnation of God's holy will of love and yet also to face it and accept it, to face and accept it because it *is* love which is thus dealing with us, a love which while condemning does not let us go but holds us to itself 'just as we are', is to move into an entirely new relation to God, a relation of 'sincere and true penitence in His presence'. But it is also and at the same time to move into a new relation of being forgiven and knowing that you are forgiven of God. As the sinner casts himself in penitence and faith 'just as he is' on this divine, holy love which has come to him in Christ, it is given to him of God to know that he is accepted and received, like the prodigal son in the parable, and the profound separation and alienation of his being from God, sinful as it is, is removed. These two things, penitence and the sense of forgiveness—both grounded in the revelation in Christ—though distinguishable in reflection and statement, are given together in a single, inclusive, ultimate

[7] 1 *John* 4, 18.

personal relation, the penitence being the deeper and more sincere because the holy love of God is apprehended as forgiving, the forgiveness being apprehended as the more overwhelming and amazing, calling for a total commitment of the self to it, the more the sinner, in his penitence, feels his utter unworthiness of it and his utter need for it.

Yet, of course, thus to state these things in abstract terms and general propositions is inevitably to be remote from the living heart of the matter. Second order abstract terms and general propositions are never adequate to, always in a measure misrepresent, first order personal relations. It is, we repeat, Christ's vocation as Reconciler to meet us, in the midst of our concrete personal existence, as veritably the holy will of the personal God, evoking in us a sincere and true penitence in the sense in which we have defined those terms, and at the same time mediating the divine forgiveness which meets that penitence, and meeting it makes it sincerer and truer; but the encounter itself is obviously much more than is or can be contained in such statements. This is borne witness to by the fact that the deepest experience of Christ's reconciling work in this matter has from the beginning always been centred in the Passion and the Cross. No one can hope to compass in thought and word that most dread happening in history in all the concrete actuality of its happening—what it meant and means to Christ, what it meant and means to God, and even—to bring it nearer to ourselves—what it has meant and means to men and women who have found in it and continue to find in it an overwhelming apocalypse of the divine condemning and pardoning love which holds them and will not let them go. We are here in the presence of one of the ultimate mysteries of being, of the divine-human personal order. In particular we are in the presence of the ultimate mystery of the person of Christ, the *mysterium Christi*. That in Christ there meets us not merely a superlatively good man shaming and challenging us, but the veritable holy love of God Himself savingly dealing with us in our sinfulness, laying hold of mind and heart and conscience in an ultimate divine-human personal relation of judgment and forgiveness that is a proposition which, if it be true, can only be known to be true in living experience of the reality itself. If God thus encounters and deals with us in Christ, well then, so He encounters and deals with us, and behind that it is not possible to go to anything deeper and more ultimate.

(8)

There is, however, a difficulty in the line of thought we have been pursuing which some may feel and on which a word may be said. It may be objected that if God's forgiveness is thus bound up with our being sincerely and truly penitent towards Him, how then can anyone hope to receive it? For how can a sinful man ever achieve such a penitence? And further, it is said, if divine forgiveness is conditional upon our being sincerely and truly penitent, shall we not be found feverishly examining ourselves to see whether our penitence really conforms to that description, and shall we not be found perhaps trying to work ourselves up to the right sort and degree of penitence and so in effect earning our forgiveness? Thus we shall not find reconciliation and peace, but once again only effort and strain. The answer to this is to point out that we have not said that before God can forgive a *perfect* penitence must be offered to Him. Certainly, if that were the condition,

F

none could hope to be forgiven. It is part of our sinful state that we cannot offer perfect penitence; to offer it we should need first to become sinless. No, what I have said is that what is required of us is a sincere and true penitence and I have defined 'sincere' as signifying a penitence not artificially wrought up but arising out of genuine perception of the truth, and 'true' as signifying a penitence according to God's standards of judgment and not according to man's. In other words, it is a penitence which in a new and critical way has moved, so to say, into God's world out of the false and falsifying human world of sin. Without some such movement into God's world it is meaningless to speak of God receiving the sinner into *restored fellowship* with himself; given it, God can and does so receive him sinful as he is and imperfect as is his penitence. The important and decisive thing is to be now in 'God's world'. And when a man realizes that his penitence is far from being what it ought to be, even though he is now in a quite new way through Christ in God's world —indeed it is only because he is thus in God's world that he realizes that his penitence, however deeply felt, is far from being what it ought to be—what is then required of him is not to try to work himself up to an even greater intensity of feeling, but simply to be humbly penitent that he is not, as he well knows, penitent enough, to accept humbly God's judgment on such poor penitence as he is able, even in the presence of the holy love manifested in the Cross, to offer, and to commit himself in faith to that same love and the forgiveness it offers. Thus it is not the perfection of our penitence which saves us, but once more God's free forgiving grace and the faith which it evokes; yet, as Calvin insisted, it is a faith which has at its heart penitence, and a penitence which has at its heart faith and self-commitment to God. Thus faith and penitence are not to be separated from one another.[8]

(9)

We turn now to the second strand of thought which, we said, meets us in the history of reflection on the atoning work of Christ, the thought, namely, that something in addition to the sinner's penitence is necessary if he is to be forgiven. It will be recalled that I said that in the Gospels this second strand is hinted at in our Lord's thought of his death as in some sense a representative offering to God on behalf of sinful men, and also that the same thought is to be met elsewhere in the New Testament. In neither case, however, is there any clear lead given how this is to be understood. I want to propose an interpretation of it which, following the line I briefly indicated,[9] may help to bring the two contrasted elements into a discernible unity with one another.

We must ask, what is the deep, abiding truth which underlies and comes to expression in the conviction, traceable throughout the history of religion, that man's sin can as it were be covered up, neutralized, by the offering of a sacrifice, the more costly the sacrifice the more adequate and effective the covering; so that the sacrifice having been made, the sinner, his sin being thus now covered, may present himself before, and be received of, God? The answer to this question, I suggest, is to be primarily sought in the fundamental awareness of all living religion that God meets man and discloses Himself as God to him in and through an absolute demand or

[8] Calvin, *Institutes*, Bk. 3, Ch. 3.
[9] See above, p. 59.

claim upon him. This may be expressed in another way by saying that there is in all living religion some awareness, however rudimentary or dim or even perverted, that the basis of all right relation to God is unconditional obedience, and that the source of all estrangement from God, the very essence of sin, is refusal to yield such obedience. If this be so, it is not difficult to understand why the idea of sacrifice has been and is so central in religion. In the sacrificial rite, most clearly perhaps in the offering up of a living victim, there is an acknowledgment, in concrete, symbolic, costing act, of God's absolute claim to man's obedience. And if we ask, why should sacrifice, especially costing sacrifice, be understood as necessary to cover sin already committed, so that by it a man is made fit to enter into the divine presence, the answer lies in the necessity the sinner feels to be laid upon him to acknowledge God's right to obedience with, as it were, the greater emphasis because in the sin that is being covered that right had in fact been flouted and denied. If the source of his estrangement from God is his refusal to yield to God's absolute claim upon him then the condition of reconciliation to God must be an acknowledgment of that absolute claim with such force, or in other words at such 'sacrificial' cost, that it is now made unmistakably plain, as plain as word and deed can make it, that the sinner's former rejection of the claim is now utterly repudiated and forsworn. In other words, such costly sacrifice for sin is the fullest possible expression in external, concrete action of *penitence towards God*.

It is not easy to express the point I am here seeking to make, for the reason that it is never possible to translate into smooth propositions the living transactions of the human spirit with God, the deep feeling-intuitions which

inform them and make them 'living'. This is particularly
so in this matter of sin, penitence and forgiveness, as
indeed the symbolisms of sacrifice, especially blood-sacri-
fice, make plain. But seeking, as we must seek, for not too
inadequate words, it may help to recall the moving passage
in Anselm's *Cur Deus Homo*, wherein he asks the reader to
imagine himself standing in the immediate, living presence of God, and 'someone said to you "look there", and
God said "on the contrary I will that you on no account
look", ask your own heart what there is among all things
that are for which you would against God's will give that
look.'[10] Thus he brings out the absoluteness of the religious
man's sense of God's claim and right to obedience. The
remainder of the treatise is built up on the principle which
Anselm takes to be self-evident that the sinner's flouting
of God's right to absolute obedience requires a repudiation which comprises within itself the costing absoluteness
which has hitherto been lacking. This is wrought out in
a doctrine of Christ's atoning work which is in many ways
unsatisfactory, but it is not the doctrine we are interested
in here, but rather the impressive setting forth of the
principle on which it rests.

In all this nothing has been said about a vicarious or
representative 'covering sacrifice' for sin; yet this also, as
we have said, is a concept traceable throughout the history
of religion. What then lies behind and finds expression in
it? To us, with our highly developed, perhaps over-
developed sense of individuality, it might seem self-
evident that only a man's own offered sacrifice, only his
own costing acknowledgment of God's absolute claim
upon him, could be thought to cover his disobediences.
But we must remind ourselves that historically living

[10] *Loc. cit.*

religion has always been essentially as much a community concern as a concern of the individual; indeed, on its more primitive levels it would appear to have been much more exclusively such a community concern than on its later and higher levels. Professor John Macmurray has gone so far as to say that the essential function of religion is to create, maintain, express and extend the community of persons, the emotional relations which unite the members of a group;[11] and though we may not wish to express the point in such an unqualified way, the general truth is beyond question. Only in the light of it can we even begin to penetrate to the experience and insight which has underlain, and underlies, the notion of representative sacrifice for sin. Sin, being deeply felt to be a community concern, the covering of it, the 'expiation' of it before God is as deeply felt to be a community concern needing to be implemented and expressed in some sort of representative, community, sacrificial act, whether in the form of the pouring out of the blood of a representative, sacrificial victim or in some other way.

(10)

Returning now to the New Testament thought of Christ's death on the Cross as in some sense a representative sacrifice for sin, my suggestion is that we can go at least some way in the understanding of it by following fundamentally the same line of thought as that just indicated, with, however, this crucial (almost quite literally *crucial*) difference that the truths involved are now

[11] J. Macmurray, *The Structure of Religious Experience* (London, Faber and Faber, 1936), *passim*.

radically re-interpreted and transformed by God's new revelation of himself as holy love which he has given in Christ, supremely in the death on the Cross.

Through the revelation in Christ God's requirement of man is given a new and final content; it is now shown to be the demand for an unqualified trust as well as an unqualified obedience (utter trust in obedience, utter obedience in trust) manifesting itself in a selfless and un-reckoning love to men. In Christ, and supremely in his Cross, these things find expression in the most absolute form. The New Testament speaks more than once of the complete obedience and self-offering to God manifested in his going to the Cross. 'He became obedient unto death, even the death of the cross.'[12] 'By the obedience of one shall many be made righteous.'[13] 'He learned obedience by the things which he suffered.'[14] In the great passage in the tenth chapter of Hebrews Christ's obedience is ex-plicitly related to the concept of sacrifice itself.[15] And all this is clearly reflected in the Gospel picture of Christ. The word 'obedience' or an equivalent term is not there used, but the essential meaning of the term is present through-out, most of all in the spirit of utter dedication which breathes through the account of his going up to Jerusalem to Calvary and, very particularly, of the agony in the Garden—'Nevertheless not my will, but thine be done.'[16] Yet also, and just as much, the New Testament teaches that if Christ went to the Cross out of obedience to God, he went also out of an infinite love to men, these two being inseparable from one another; furthermore, that in this obedience and trust towards God and love towards

---

[12] *Philippians* 2, 8. [13] *Romans* 5, 19.
[14] *Hebrews* 5, 8. [15] *Hebrews* 10, 5–12.
[16] *Luke* 22, 42.

men there was manifest in him the full and unsullied perfection of human personal life.[17]

In the Cross, then, there meets us livingly and in action
the perfection of human personal life which towards God
is absolute obedience and trust and towards men is
absolute love, the absoluteness in both cases being finally
demonstrated (by the logic of divine-human relations
which the Apostle Paul sets forth in the fifth chapter of
Romans) by Christ's total yielding up of himself to God in
a death, at the hands of sinful men, of the most appalling
agony and loneliness and shame. At the same time and by
the same token the Cross utterly exposes man's sinful
disobedience and distrust towards God and lovelessness
towards his fellows. All this makes possible, and, as it lays
hold of a man, makes actual, a new sort of penitence, a
sincere and true penitence of the kind we have set forth
earlier. The sinner, discerning these things, is now in the
real world, God's world, in a way in which hitherto, because of his sin-induced blindness, he has not been, and
in which he could not now be apart from Christ.

(11)

But the question remains: how and in what sense this
costly self-offering and obedience of Christ, which reveals
to a man the real nature of his sin, can be thought of as
'covering' it, so that at one and the same time the penitent
man is enabled to stand before God both condemned and
at peace. In seeking the answer to this we may refer again
to the fifth chapter of Romans. In this chapter the
Apostle appears to be working, admittedly in a somewhat
baffling way, with the concept of 'solidarity'. Following,

[17] E.g *Galatians* 2, 20; *Romans* 5, 8; 8, 35; *Ephesians* 4, 13; *Hebrews* 4, 15.

apparently, Rabbinical teaching he draws a parallel between the effects of the sinful disobedience of the one man
Adam as extending to the whole race of mankind and
the effects of the perfect obedience of the one man Christ
as extending to a whole new race of mankind which God
has brought, and is bringing, into being by the latter's
sacrificial death. The Apostle leaves this notion of solidarity, which as we have seen runs, in one form or another, through the history of religion, particularly in
association with sacrifice, in considerable obscurity; but
he gives us a lead which may serve our thought here and
at the same time illustrate once again how the revelation
in Christ completely transforms and re-interprets men's
religious ideas. The lead is to be found in the frequent
reference throughout the whole chapter to the divine
grace—the 'free gift of grace', 'grace reigning', 'grace
abounding through Christ', 'the sphere of grace in which
we stand'. Though there is but one explicit reference to the
'grace of the one man, Christ Jesus',[18] clearly the whole
chapter is dominated by the thought of the divine grace
manifested in Christ. What then does 'grace' here mean?
Plainly it means basically the going forth through Christ
of the divine love, the divine *agapé*, in free, unmerited, self-
giving, self-revealing, saving action towards sinful men.
In other words, the somewhat impersonal idea of 'solidarity' is in the Apostle's thought continuously taken up
into, merged in, transformed and informed by the deeper
and more personal concept of a union between Christ and
the sinner brought about and constituted by Christ's pure
and perfect love on the one hand and the sinner's response
in the penitence and self-commitment which that love
evokes on the other.

[18] v. 15 (N.E.B.).

How then, and in what sense, we ask again, can the sinner's sin be meaningfully said to be covered by Christ's obedience and self-offering on the Cross? I do not find it easy to express what, in the light of what has just been said and of my own experience such as it is, I believe the answer to be. But perhaps it is best expressed along lines similar to those followed by McLeod Campbell in his still in many ways unsurpassed book *The Nature of the Atonement*. Standing before the Cross, the sinner utters a heartfelt 'Amen' to its perfect obedience and trust, its perfect self-offering and sacrifice to God, and also at the same time to its utter condemnation and repudiation of his own disobedience and lovelessness now laid bare. Though himself unable to offer to God anything that even approaches perfect obedience and trust and love to men, he is able in a very real sense to identify himself with Christ's perfect obedience and trust and love, to say 'Amen' to it, with his whole being, even though he knows he cannot in fact in his sinfulness yield up his whole being in a like perfect way. And he is enabled and entitled to do this, to take as it were Christ's offering and sacrifice of himself on the Cross and 'cover' himself under it, offer himself however imperfectly under its cover, because the perfect love manifested in the offering and sacrifice is holding him to itself, refusing to let him go. This it seems to me constitutes, for the sinner, even in his sinfulness, an entirely new relation to God, the relation of sincere and deep penitence (including penitence for not being penitent enough) and trustful self-commitment. And it is all 'through Christ', and supremely through his death on the Cross.

I am conscious of the clumsy inadequacy of these statements; yet I am constrained to think that they do express and represent, however fumblingly, something of what has lain at the heart of the Christian experience of forgiveness through the death of Christ all down the ages. There have of course been many varying expressions of this experience; but they all seek in one way or another to convey the truth that the sinner is called, and enabled, to stand 'just as he is' in the presence of God alongside the crucified One, to be penitent in a new and deep way because of so standing, and to offer himself to God not in his own perfect obedience and trust, for these he knows he cannot command, but 'in Christ' who loved him and gave himself for him. And to him, so standing, there is given the assurance and peace of forgiveness, of reconciliation with God. He is, in St Paul's words, 'at peace with God through our Lord Jesus Christ, through whom we have been allowed to enter the sphere of God's grace, where we now stand.'[19]

(12)

And now it is to be observed in conclusion that this line of thought, vague and unsatisfactory as it may be in content and expression, puts at the heart and centre of our Lord's reconciling work a dominant *Godward* reference and movement. The work of Christ in evoking in men a sincere and true and continually renewed penitence, so that they are able to utter a deeply felt 'Amen' to his perfect obedience and love, including its searching condemnation of themselves, could only be accomplished under the form of an offering to God. For it was accomplished, and in the nature of the case had to be accomplished, under the form of the perfect human life,

[19] *Romans* 5, 1 (N.E.B.).

and the form of the perfect human life is the completest offering of itself to God. If it is not thus wholly Godward in its direction, it is not the perfect human life. There is therefore nothing mysterious or calling for a special corresponding factor in our doctrine of the Atonement that when our Lord's life was mounting to its awful climax on the Cross, he should think of his death as being at one and the same time both offered to God and on behalf of men. Furthermore, the reconciling work of Christ in this sphere is, as we have said, to bring men to a sincere and true penitence *towards God*, to a new self-commitment in humble trust *towards God*, to the profoundest possible re-orientation of their whole being and life *towards God*. Once again the primary and central and all-controlling reference is necessarily Godward. Christ's priestly work is thus wholly Godward; yet also and by the same token it is wholly manward, for it is not possible to obey God without perfectly loving men, God being what he is in his nature and purpose. Christ reconciles man to God by giving him a new mind, a *metanoia*, of sincere and true penitence and faith, but he can only thus radically change him by a saving work which begins, continues and ends in a Godward movement of his own pure and mighty spirit.

CHAPTER IV

CHRIST'S OFFICE AS KING

WHEN we use the symbol 'king' in relation to Christ's vocation as Reconciler we have basically in mind that which comes to expression in the New Testament in the confession that 'Jesus is Lord'.[1] The symbol sums up the truth that it is essential to Christ's saving and reconciling work that he establishes himself in the life of the believer as being in himself, in some objectively real and not merely metaphorical or 'as if' sense, that sovereign, personal, holy will of God to which the absolute surrender and obedience of the whole person is due, with which in the end all accounts must be settled, to which alone belong 'the kingdom, the power and the glory'. Or to put it in terms of the distinctive New Testament apprehension of the 'kingdom', to speak of the kingship of Christ is another way of describing the eschatological faith that in Christ God himself is at work in the world and in human life and history in a new and decisive way, has initiated a new, effective and victorious action in relation to evil, which action will at the last be consummated and completed in a fashion that transcends and transforms this present world as we now know it. Christ, according to the New Testament, is the centre and source and bearer of this divine saving initiative and activity in the world; in him and through him redeemed men and women are

[1] I *Corinthians* 12, 3.

taken up into that activity, become one with it; they become the willing subjects of the divine kingdom, and are destined to participate in its final victory—the rule and victory of Christ, which are the rule and victory of God.

If now we seek to explore more fully what in Christ's reconciling work is thus summed up in the symbol of his kingship, we may do so along three lines.

(1)

The first has to do with something which happens in the sphere of the will of the individual believer. It is an essential element in the saving, reconciling work of Christ in a man's life that he evokes and sustains an attitude of willed submission to himself in which is acknowledged the obligation of unconditional obedience to whatever may be discerned to be his mind and will. In an older and once more familiar evangelical phraseology this attitude was variously described as 'decision for Christ', 'giving the heart to Christ', 'full surrender' and so on. No doubt some dubious theology and some dubious methods of preaching and evangelism were at times associated with these and similar phrases, but they rightly point to the living heart and centre of the distinctively new life they have in view, namely that a man must recognize in Christ the unconditional, absolute, final, sacred directive of life and conduct.

The point is, I suppose, obvious enough; yet it is not unimportant to state it with an explicit emphasis on the submission of the *will*. For there is always perhaps some danger, especially for certain temperaments, that Christian piety and discipleship will take the form of an emotionalism in which fervid feelings towards Christ (apprehended as

likely as not through a highly sentimentalized picture of
him) are assumed to be the infallible and indispensable
sign of the truly redeemed life, and accordingly cultivated.
One has on occasion met this sort of piety which seems to
measure the depth and reality of its faith by the sheerly
emotional intensity with which it can speak of 'dear
Jesus' or can sing, in words reminiscent of a love-lyric or a
love-letter, 'I am his and he is mine for ever and for ever.'
And one has, alas, noticed that at times this 'Jesus-cult'
accompanies a sadly narrow and uninspired convention-
ality of conduct. One is not suggesting for one moment,
of course, that there is no place for feeling, deep feeling, in the Christian life, and not least for feelings of
humble gratitude to God for his coming in Christ 'for us
men and our salvation'. The point is simply that the sort
of emotionalism I have in mind is stuffy and debilitating
and is not the truth of the reconciled man's relation to
Christ as this is exhibited to us in the New Testament. In
the true relation there is assuredly something much sharp-
er, more austere, something as it were more astringent
and acidic, something more imperial, something in short
corresponding to the thought of Christ as king, *Christus
Imperator*. Christ does not save a man by bringing him
into a hot-house where there bloom in a heavy and
humid air exotic, not to say erotic, flowers of piety, but
rather by calling him to be out with him on the slopes of a
mountain-range where there is a keen air and the climb
up is stiff enough to call out every ounce of spiritual and
moral vigour and courage and decision and determination that he can muster. We merely change the metaphor
again when we say that Christ is, in addition to all else
that may be said about him, *King*. He claims to rule the
will and direct the deed absolutely, and only so far as that

claim is continuously acknowledged can his full reconciling and saving work in a man's life be accomplished.

(2)

It is important, however, rightly to understand what sort of kingly authority this is which is thus ascribed to Christ. It is properly symbolized under the image of 'king' because, as has just been said, the reconciled man is constrained to acknowledge that Christ is entitled to his absolute obedience and that everything must be brought into subjection to his will;[2] but the word 'absolute' here must obviously not be misinterpreted. It signifies no more than that the will of Christ is in principle accepted as conclusive whatever may be the difficulties and dubieties amidst the confusions and perplexities of practical life of discerning what it requires: nothing else whatever is to be put into the balance with it. But it is not absolute in the sense of being overridingly dictatorial, requiring a literalistic and legalistic, a merely slavish and uncomprehending subjection to commands or rules or injunctions whether these be in the form of sayings recorded in the Gospels or in the form of instructions from an ecclesiastical or other sort of authority claiming to speak in his name. This is but to repeat what has earlier been said more than once, particularly in the discussion of Christ's office as prophet;[3] but the repetition is worth while because it affords further illustration of the necessity not to separate the three offices of Christ from one another: the kingly office must at this point be strictly interpreted in the light of the prophetic and priestly offices. All Christ's teaching and manner of life, all his dealings with men and women, and

Cf. 2 *Corinthians* 10, 5.   [3] See above, pp. 41, 46–48.

above all the Cross through which there shines forth with
such piercing and cleansing power the judging and forgiving love of God, show that in the new life into which a
man is lifted by Christ any sort of merely coercive, dictatorial overriding authority can have no place. The only
sort of obedience which is in place is one which all the
time expresses loyalty to a man's own insight, a Christ-
illumined insight, of course, but none the less his own.
There is no contrariety between saying that the reconciled
man acknowledges Christ's rule as absolute and saying that
that rule is mediated to him through his own judgment;
so far from there being any contrariety the two things are
inseparably bound up together. It is indeed almost a
commonplace that it is only by being resolutely obedient
to what we ourselves can discern of the mind of Christ,
however poor that discernment may be, that we become
more sensitively aware of what that mind is. And, furthermore, it is precisely the conviction that in Christ there
meets us God's final word to us to which, as we are able
to grasp it, an absolute obedience is due, which plays an
important, indeed indispensable part in quickening our
own personal insight and vision—this in two ways.

(3)

First, there are few things more paralysing to, more in-
hibiting of, the higher insights of a man's spirit, more calculated to make him lose all clear sense of direction and
so yield insensibly and increasingly to a policy of drift, inclination and acquiescence than to lose the sense that
there is anywhere accessible to him a moral absolute
which is not to be trifled with and on which the whole
being can and ought to be staked in obedience and trust.

That appears to be the position of multitudes today; they are bogged down in moral relativism. Such a relativism, the feeling that there is no firm standing ground anywhere for the human spirit in its crucial choices and decisions, no, as it were, supporting and reliable moral environment, weakens the capacity both for moral perception and moral loyalty, for it can offer but little resistance to the reduction of morals to group customs and conventions and to a utilitarianism which conforms to such customs and conventions only so far as prudence or profit may be thought to dictate. It is, therefore, not the least thing that Christ does savingly for a man that he establishes himself in the innermost places of his being as 'king', establishes himself amidst the flux of personal impulses and desires as well as amidst the powerful and persistent pressures of the group, as an absolute, an unconditional for the will, not deriving merely from the man himself or from his group. It is not the least thing that Christ does savingly for a man that he imparts the sense, continually renewed amidst all the problems and perplexities, that there *are* final principles and allegiances in the personal world and so quickens both the search after and insight into what those principles and allegiances are.

Second, by the submission of his will to Christ as *king* the reconciled man is carried a long way towards being released from that anxiety as to the future, that worrying over-concern about what may be the results and consequences of what he does in obedience to conscience, that always besetting temptation to play providence to one's own life, to live too much in the future and not enough in the immediate tasks and duties of the present taking 'no thought for the morrow', which do much to fog moral and spiritual insight and vision. We might say that the king-

ship of Christ means in effect that there is only *one* thing
committed to the reconciled man's care and that is to do
the best and the wisest according to the mind of Christ that
he can at the moment discern; all else, all the effects and
consequences of what he thus does both in his own life
and in the lives of others he is required to commit wholly
and without anxiety to Christ. This has the sound perhaps
of a sermonic truism, but it in fact expresses an important
and unique aspect of Christ's reconciling work.

There is, indeed, a platitudinous piece of advice, often
given, which bids men just to do their best in any given
situation and not waste nervous energy in worrying about
things over which they have no control. 'Do your best, the
best can do no more.' But to suppose that this is all we have
in mind here is to miss the point. We are not here thinking
of a merely secular, commonsense, and somewhat obvious
wisdom of life, but of religious belief and in particular of
Christian belief; not of the futility of anxiety and worry,
but of a deep self-commitment of faith; not of the cultiva-
tion of a resigned acceptance of whatever life, with its
incalculable vicissitudes and insecurities, may bring forth
in spite of all our planning, but of a deep *peace* of mind
which the Apostle Paul describes as 'passing all understanding', as 'of God' and as 'through Christ Jesus'.[4]
The meaning of these pregnant phrases in the Apostle's
thought can only be grasped in the light of his whole faith,
his whole Christology, as these meet us throughout his
epistles; but one central element in that faith and Christology can properly be expressed for the purposes of our
thought here in the symbol and figure of Christ as the
King (even though the Apostle does not himself use the
term), who not only claims obedience but also holds all

[4] *Philippians* 4, 7.

things, including all that may flow by way of consequence from obedience, in the grasp of his ruling and over-ruling wisdom and power and love.[5]

Two things may be added. First: to say, as we have done, that the only thing committed to the care of the reconciled man is to do the best and the wisest according to the mind of Christ which he can at the moment discern, all else being committed to Christ as king, does not imply that the estimation of the possible or probable consequences of various lines of conduct open to him should not enter into the determination of his conduct, into the determination of what the mind and will of Christ for him are. That would be absurd. The call to obey Christ is certainly not a call to act blindly and irresponsibly without exercising such foresight and forethought as a man can command, to act merely from impressionistic feeling-judgments and subconscious 'hunches'. But it does imply that there may at any moment enter into the reconciled man's practical conduct of life, into his choices and decisions, a more direct sense of what obedience to Christ requires of him or forbids to him, a sense, that is to say, which does not spring merely from the calculation of consequences and cannot be justified on that basis, but from the revelation God has made of himself in Christ and from the call to bear witness to that revelation by a new and distinctive Christ-style of life in the midst of mankind, whatever the consequences of so doing may be. Second,

[5] It is not necessary to substantiate this by detailed references and exposition. No one can peruse the pages of the New Testament without discerning how the new and reconciled life therein set forth is dominated by the thought of the Kingship of Christ. It may be noted that the line of thought pursued above has brought us back by another route and from another angle to what was said in the first lecture about reconciliation to God's requirements and God's appointments.

what we have said does not imply that the Christian man is saved from mistaken judgments, from misapprehending what the will of Christ for him is. Because, as has been said, Christ's rule is not of the authoritarian, overriding kind, the reconciled man has to grow in insight and discernment; but the mistakes and misjudgments he makes he is entitled to believe, by virtue of his faith in the kingship of Christ, are never abortive and sterile; they are taken up into and turned into account by the saving and ruling purpose of Christ the King in his own life and in the lives of others.

(4)

The second aspect of Christ's reconciling work which we subsume under the symbol of his kingship is concerned with the Church. It is today superfluous to insist that the doctrine of the Church in New Testament experience and thought is central, deep and far-reaching,[6] but for our particular interest here, namely, its connection with the kingship of Christ, we may treat it with a brevity which might otherwise seem to be disproportionate.

We may recall the fourth of the four aspects of the life of reconciliation to God through Christ which we set forth in the first chapter, namely, that the reconciled man is brought into a new order of relations with other persons. Now the New Testament makes it abundantly plain that it is an essential and central part of this new order of persons-in-relation that the reconciled man is incorporated

[6] 'Christian theology', writes Prof. John Knox in a recent book which is to be commended as a singularly powerful and illuminating treatment of its theme, 'in the present epoch is marked, perhaps most distinctively, by concern for the nature and importance of the Church.' (*The Church and the Reality of Christ*—London, Collins, 1963, p. 9.)

into a new and distinctive community of which Christ
is, and is continuously apprehended by its members to
be, the sustaining, constitutive, indwelling, unifying, all-
directing principle of its being and life. It is this acknowledged common relation of all the members, both in-
dividually and corporately, to the one living, ascended and
ever-present Lord that once and for all and *toto coelo* dif-
ferentiates the Christian church from all other groups of
persons whatsoever and explains and justifies the application of the word 'holy' to it in its creed. The Church is
holy and is conscious of itself as such not, needless to say,
because it is perfect or supposes itself to be perfect, but
because, for all its sins and imperfections, it has in fact
been brought into being, is sustained in being, and draws
thence all its new and distinctive life, by the divine
Redeemer who is its living head and king. It is important
for our purpose in these lectures to note that both the
prophetic and the priestly offices of Christ enter into and
are inseparably bound up with this distinctive life of the
Christian fellowship which Christ thus creates, constitutes
and rules. The three offices, as always, 'co-inhere', if one
may use the term. Thus the saving truth he brings in his
office as prophet is given in ever-fuller reach and depth
only through the fellowship—to use the New Testament
phrases, it is only with all Christ's people that we may
grasp what is the breadth and length and height and depth
of the love of Christ, may know it though it is beyond
knowledge.[7] The pardon and peace which he brings to
sinful men through his offering of himself to God on the
Cross, that is, in his priestly office, are continually renewed in the worship of the Church, the preaching of the
'word of the gospel' and above all in the sacrament of

[7] *Ephesians* 3, 18–19 (N.E.B.).

Holy Communion, the community-meal which he himself instituted, at which he himself is present and presides, and through whose elements and acts there is set forth in powerful, yet simple, symbols the fact of his 'dying for our sins' and the benefits which flow from this for his people.

A further minor point may be added. The aspect of Christ's kingly office of which we are now speaking, namely, his headship over the redeemed community, the Church, is obviously not separate from his rule in the life of the individual believer of which we spoke earlier in this lecture, nor from his sovereignty over the cosmos of which we shall go on to speak next. The one symbol of 'king' is appropriate throughout. Nevertheless the community reference may be thought to impart to the symbol a special fitness. The New Testament uses a variety of figures to express Christ's all-controlling relation to his Church and its members, e.g. the figure of the head and the body, of the vine and its branches, of the cornerstone of a building, but the word 'king' in its ordinary usage has always connoted and to most minds still connotes an office which has pre-eminence and bears authority primarily in relation to a community and only by extension to other things.

(5)

We turn now to the third aspect of Christ's reconciling work which comes to expression in the symbol of his kingship; it has a still wider, indeed the widest possible reference—a cosmic reference. It has been fundamental to our whole treatment of Christ's reconciling work that in him there meets us in and through concrete, historical personal reality the love of God; the primary emphasis has therefore inevitably tended to be on the revelation of God as *love* and all that that means; but it now falls, as we think of Christ's office as king, more on the term *God*, and particularly on that which might be said to be, religiously, the central element in the idea of God, namely, his final and absolute sovereignty. The love of God, being of *God*, is necessarily a love which is regnant over all, including all that is evil and opposed to it; to it belong 'the kingdom, the power and the glory'. From this it follows that if the same love is incarnate and savingly at work in Christ, then to Christ belong 'the kingdom, the power and the glory' also. Christ therefore for Christian faith is 'king', not only as already said in relation to the individual believer and to the redeemed community, but also in relation to the whole created order and the fulfilment of God's purpose in it. This stupendous thought occurs more than once in more or less explicit terms in the New Testament. Christ's cosmic Lordship is indeed thought of as being wholly 'under God', but it is not any the less Lordship for being thus God intended and God given. 'It pleased the Father . . . by him to reconcile all things unto himself; by him, I say, whether they be things in earth or things in heaven.' 'That in the dispensation of the fulness of times he might gather together in one all things in Christ, both which are in heaven, and which are on earth.' 'For he must reign, till he (God) hath put all enemies under his feet.'[8]

This aspect of the kingship of Christ obviously connects with what was said earlier in these chapters about the relation of eschatological faith to the reconciled life. We have indicated at more than one point how faith in the Lordship of Christ as bound up with the final establish-

[8] *Colossians* 1, 20; *Ephesians* 1, 10; 1 *Corinthians* 15, 25. See also *Philippians* 2, 10.

ment of the Kingdom of God is an essential element in the Christian experience of reconciliation and there is no need to cover the ground again.[9] There is, however, an important point, which I have not hitherto referred to, and on which it is worth while to say a word. It has to do with the forgiveness of sins, with that distinctive work of Christ whereby he makes a man poignantly conscious of his sinfulness in the presence of God and yet at the same time sets him at peace about it; more particularly it has to do with the consequences of a man's sin in the lives of other men and women for whom Christ, as part of his saving work for us and in us, teaches us to have deep concern.

I recall once being asked the question, not in a merely theoretical way, but manifestly as a real *cri de cœur*: how can I, how dare I, be at peace about my sins, how can I rightly accept God's forgiveness, when the consequences of my past evil living are still unfolding in the lives of others before my very eyes, utterly beyond my control and restitution? If we may high-light the question by glaring examples, to the like of which however it must not by any means be restricted, what right has the seducer, however penitent, to be at peace when the life of the one he seduced is still perverted and wrecked? Or what right can the drunkard or gambler, however contrite, have to peace in the presence of God when his wife and children are still paying heavy penalties for his wrong-doing? There is no answer to such questions unless it is given to the repentant man to know that in Christ there has met him and meets him not merely a holy love which judges and pardons but one which is also *sovereign*, which holds all men and *all*

[9] See above, pp. 27 ff., 39. See also my *The World and God* (London, James Nisbet & Co. Ltd, 1935), Ch. 12.

G*

things within the firm grasp of its redeeming purpose, and which therefore holds in that same grasp all the consequences of our sin in the lives of others. At this point Christ's office as king enters indispensably into his office as priest; we glimpse again the unity of 'the offices', the 'seamless robe' of his vocation as Reconciler.

(6)

We turn now to another and somewhat puzzling element in this cosmic aspect of Christ's office as king. It is one which we may best approach by taking note of what has been called the 'classical' view of the Atonement, the view, that is to say, which speaks of Christ's saving work as a victory won supremely through his Cross and resurrection over all the powers of evil which apparently hold man in bondage, such powers being pictured as quasi-personal powers or beings, sometimes as a single power or being—Satan.[10] Aulen denominates this way of depicting Christ's saving work 'classical' because it was apparently dominant throughout the early centuries of the Church, having its roots in the New Testament itself. In the latter there is mysterious reference more than once to the dominance of 'principalities' and 'powers' (*archai* and *exousiai*) over the world and mankind, which dominance Christ overthrew.[11]

How are we to interpret this from the point of view of our special interest in these chapters?

It may be suggested that we must distinguish between two questions. There is, first, the question how the general idea of a victory won by Christ once and for all through his

[10] G. Aulen, *Christus Victor* (London, S.P.C.K., 1931), pp. 20 ff.
[11] E.g. *Colossians* 2, 15 and 20; *Romans* 8, 38; *Ephesians* 1, 21; 3, 10; 6, 12.

Cross and resurrection over powers of evil in the cosmos is related to the Christian man's reconciliation to God. Does the idea correspond with and express something central and fundamental in the reconciled life, in what Christ as Reconciler does for us? The answer is surely that it does. We must call to mind the immense and frightening power and weight and resistance of evil in human history and life, its continuous penetration into the remotest corners of man's existence, its unceasing moulding of every new generation into conformity with itself; we must form, if we can, a single picture of it in all its hideous, concrete actuality as it were *en masse*. To form such a massive picture and to feel at least occasionally profoundly distressed by it is, in these tragic days, not difficult for any man of even average sensibility. But for the man of specifically Christian sensibility, one that is, who is learning—in the Apostle's phrase—to 'put on Christ', to have his mind, to yearn for the things he stood for, above all to *love* men and women with at least something of the all-embracing *agapé* of God which was incarnate in him, for such an one the awareness of the unrelieved and apparently undiminishing evil of human life would be too burdensome to be borne were there nothing more to be said. But there is something more to be said. As the Christian man confronts all this weight of evil, feels the burden, *la peine forte et dure*, of it pressing upon him, feels the burden of it precisely because he has been taught by Christ thus to feel the burden of it, it is an immense and indeed indispensable element in his reconciliation and peace to know that something victoriously effective was accomplished once and for all by the Saviour, that evil, despite all appearance to the contrary, has been defeated and overthrown, the strong man bound, the rot stopped, whatever metaphor he may care to use. In stating this we are stating a familiar and tested truth of the Christian experience of reconciliation. To any one who brings to the evil of the world and of human life a Christ-sensitized imagination and love, it makes all the difference in the world to be able to put it to himself, that in Christ God *has* actively met and conquered evil once for all on a cosmic scale in a conclusive act of victorious love and power; so that Christ's word on the Cross 'it is finished' may be taken to mean that his victory over evil was now accomplished, or to use the word 'finished' in a more colloquial sense, it was evil that was 'finished' once for all. 'The strife is o'er, the battle done; now is the Victor's triumph won—Alleluia!'

(7)

The other question which arises in relation to the New Testament affirmation of Christ's victory over evil is concerned with the form in which the affirmation is expressed, namely, as a victory won over quasi-personal maleficent powers which in some fashion hold the world and mankind in thrall. The significance of the phrase 'principalities and powers' is a difficult problem in New Testament exegesis, but whatever conclusion is reached, the important question for us is what meaning is to be attached to it in respect of the Christian man's personal experience of Christ's reconciling work, his own entering into and receiving the benefits of that work. This question calls for an answer whether we take the phrase to signify, as it certainly did signify for the New Testament writers, the existence of real spiritual beings, powers of evil, over whom Christ won some sort of victory, or whether we take it as no more than an expression in dramatic, mythological form of the complete adequacy of Christ's saving work to overcome every evil which perverts and degrades man and prevents him from entering into his highest personal life with God. If we take the former, more literalist view, the difficulty is to form any idea how exactly Christ's victory over them was once and for all won through his Cross and resurrection, the more so in view of the fact already referred to that the evils to which the principalities and powers are believed to stand in some sort of causative relation still so tragically persist. If, on the other hand, we take the latter metaphorical or mythological view we may then adopt and adapt a line of thought suggested by A. D. Galloway, and by so doing relate the victory ascribed to Christ more directly and intimately to the experience of reconciliation itself.[12]

Galloway's discussion is concerned with the ideas of demons and demon possession in the New Testament. He suggests that these may be taken to symbolize those things in man's life which are inimical to his status and dignity as a personal being made in the image of God. 'The essence of the demonic', he writes, 'is sheer enmity to the personal. It is that which menaces the rational intentionality of the personal from within and frustrates and stultifies it from without. It is only as a loose form of speech that we can say that the demons as they are spoken of in the New Testament, for instance, are personal creatures inhabiting nature. It is when a man has descended to a sub-personal level of behaviour, as for example in madness, that he is said to be possessed by demons. Or again, in the Epistles of St Paul, the animal desires and passions, in so far as they override the intentionality of persons and

---

[12] A. D. Galloway, *The Cosmic Christ* (London, James Nisbet & Co. Ltd, 1951), pp. 217 f.

become compulsions and obsessions, are associated with the activities of demons. Disease, obtruding upon and frustrating personal life, is regarded as the work of demons. Any force which is sub-personal in form and superhuman in power has demonic associations for the primitive mind. Whenever man encountered forces which were too great for him to control, yet too void of meaning for him to make a personal submission to them in worship, these forces came to be associated with the activities of demonic powers.'[13]

Galloway does not himself give these perhaps not very happily expressed thoughts the wider cosmic reference and application to the 'principalities and powers'. But my suggestion is that we may do so. We may interpret the 'principalities and powers' as expressing and representing, in a way parallel to that indicated by Galloway in respect of demons, those *réalités cosmiques* which appear to hold humanity in an iron grip of impersonal forces, those laws of destiny in face of which the human person's needs and struggles and aspirations as a person, *ses besoins du cœur*, seem—not any less today than in ancient times—to be utterly frustrated, futile and meaningless. Some confirmation of this interpretation may be found in the New Testament. In the New Testament, as also in later Patristic descriptions of Christ's saving work, the overcoming of death is set forth as one quite central element in Christ's victory over the powers of evil. Now death expresses and sums up more than anything else in human existence the menacing pressure of the impersonal upon man as a personal being. If death is, in fact, what it appears to be, the absolute end of the human person, then it marks the final triumph of the impersonal over the

[13] Op. cit., p. 229.

personal; on the other hand, the overcoming of death, particularly when this is interpreted, as it is in the New Testament, as being raised with Christ to eternal life, marks the final triumph of the personal over the impersonal. In accordance with this it may be observed that St Paul, whilst he does not explicitly speak of death as one of the 'powers', apparently moves in that direction at least to the extent of referring to death in a quasi-personal way as an enemy in the overcoming of which, or whom, Christ's victory and reign are consummated. 'For he must reign, till he hath put all enemies under his feet. The last enemy that shall be destroyed is death.'[14]

If we may thus interpret the 'principalities and powers' as basically signifying those facts and forces which menace man's being and life as personal and which appear to be part of the very constitution of the world, it becomes possible to speak meaningfully and indeed quite realistically of Christ having once and for all overcome them. And we may do this whatever view we may be inclined to take of their precise nature and status, or of the manner in which they will be brought under the feet of Christ in the final consummation when 'God will be all in all.'[15] For our concern has been, and is, with Christ's present overcoming of them in the life of reconciliation itself here and now, that is to say, through his vocation as our reconciler. He overcomes them by giving to those in whom his reconciling work is being accomplished a present victory over them, so that they have no longer any power to crush and overwhelm. He *reconciles* to them—really reconciles; that is to say, he does not merely enable a man stoically and fatalistically to endure, which is no true reconciliation, but rather enables him, with profound

[14] 1 *Corinthians* 15, 25 f.   [15] 1 *Corinthians* 15, 28.

inward conviction and peace, to see all as held within the sovereign grasp of the same wisdom and love as was incarnate in Christ. All this is but to state in a dull, abstract and complicated way what the Apostle Paul designates, in a single pregnant phrase, 'being more than conquerors through him that loved us' and sums up in the concluding verses of the same chapter: 'In all these things we are more than conquerors through him that loved us. For I am persuaded that neither death, nor life, nor angels, nor principalities, nor powers, nor things present, nor things to come, nor height, nor depth, nor any other creature, shall be able to separate us from the love of God, which is in Christ Jesus our Lord.'[16]

(8)

'The love of God which is in Christ Jesus our Lord'.

The Apostle's ringing words make plain that however much the fully realized Kingdom of God must utterly transcend our most daring imagination and most far-ranging speculative thought, it will be a kingdom ruled by love, love of the same order as that which was incarnate and tabernacled amongst us in the person of Jesus Christ. In the fullest and most realistic sense therefore the Kingdom will be Christ's kingdom and Christ its King. May we not think that this comes to expression in the astonishing picture in the Book of Revelation of the 'slain Lamb in the midst of the throne', the Cross of Christ and his kingly office being thus brought together in almost startling juxtaposition?[17] We must never in our thought separate the final consummation of Christ's victory in the realized, transhistorical kingdom of God from the revelation of

---

[16] *Romans* 8, 37 ff.   [17] *Revelation* 5, 6.

God's nature and purpose given in Christ in history in the days of his flesh and supremely in his Cross. If the divine Kingdom has already in some sense come in Christ (though not yet in its fulness), if the final eschatological event has already begun in his advent, then obviously, if these words are to have meaning, the essential character of the kingdom must be understood to be the same throughout. This has not always been fully realized. In some theologies the so-called state of Christ's exaltation has been so set over against the so-called state of his humiliation in the days of his flesh that it has been almost impossible to discern any continuity between them, between him who walked the earth as one who had not where to lay his head and died a criminal's death on Calvary and him who is pictured as coming on the clouds of heaven in final judgment upon and overthrow of his enemies. This cannot be right. We must indeed believe that he will put all enemies under his feet, but he will do so only as 'the slain Lamb in the midst of the throne'. When we say that Christ is king, is exalted to the right hand of power, we must take care to mean the same Christ, the same Christ as he who was lifted up on the Cross that he might draw all men unto him.

(9)

So we complete our exposition of the offices of Christ—prophet, priest, king: the three central and inseparable aspects of his one, all-inclusive vocation and work as Reconciler. The climax of the exposition in the thought of him as king points to the fact that in expounding the reconciling work of Christ we have in effect been showing how central in the Christian faith and experience is the ascription of divinity to him, in whatever way that divinity may be more theoretically and theologically explored and formulated. To be able to say all that we have said of his reconciling work, culminating in the enthronement of him as the absolute Lord of conscience and will, as the Creator, Sustainer and Head of the new redeemed community, the Church, as the Lamb exalted in the midst of the realized and consummated Kingdom of God in which all things shall be put under his feet and God be all in all—this is to be constrained, not in the interest of a merely creedal orthodoxy, but because of his own inherent power to authenticate himself to us as our reconciliation and our peace, to say 'My Lord and my God'.

> Join all the glorious names
> Of wisdom, love, and power,
> That ever mortals knew,
> That angels ever bore;
> All are too mean to speak His worth,
> Too mean to set my Saviour forth.
>
> Great Prophet of my God,
> My tongue would bless Thy Name;
> By Thee the joyful news
> Of our salvation came,—
> The joyful news of sins forgiven,
> Of hell subdued, and peace with heaven.
>
> Jesus, my great High Priest,
> Offered His blood and died;
> My guilty conscience seeks
> No sacrifice beside:
> His powerful blood did once atone,
> And now it pleads before the throne.

My dear Almighty Lord,
My Conqueror and my King,
Thy sceptre and Thy sword,
Thy reigning grace I sing:
Thine is the power: behold, I sit
In willing bonds before Thy feet.

Now let my soul arise,
And tread the tempter down:
My Captain leads me forth
To conquest and a crown:
A feeble saint shall win the day,
Though death and hell obstruct the way.[18]

[18] Isaac Watts.